C I T Y P A C K

London

By Louise Nicholson

3RD EDITION

Fodor's Travel Publications, Inc.
New York • Toronto • London • Sydney • Auckland

WWW.FODORS.COM

Contents

life 5–12

how to organize your time 13–22

top 25 sights 23–48

About this book 4

About this book

KEY TO SYMBOLS

✚	map reference on the fold-out map accompanying this book (see below)	🚌	nearest bus route
		⛴	nearest riverboat or ferry stop
✉	address	♿	facilities for visitors with disabilities
☎	telephone number	✋	admission charge
🕐	opening times	⬌	other nearby places of interest
🍴	restaurant or café on premises or nearby	❓	tours, lectures, or special events
🚇	nearest tube (underground) station	➤	indicates the page where you will find a fuller description
🚆	nearest railroad station	ℹ	tourist information

Citypack London is divided into six sections to cover the six most important aspects of your visit to London. It includes:

- The author's view of the city and its people
- Itineraries, walks, and excursions
- The top 25 sights to visit—as selected by the author
- Features on what makes the city special
- Detailed listings of restaurants, hotels, shops, and nightlife
- Practical information

In addition, easy-to-read side panels provide extra facts and snippets, highlights of places to visit, and invaluable practical advice.

CROSS-REFERENCES

To help you make the most of your visit, cross-references, indicated by ➤, show you where to find additional information about a place or subject.

MAPS

The fold-out map in the wallet at the back of the book is a comprehensive street plan of London. All the map references given in the book refer to this map. For example, the Wallace Collection, in Manchester Square, has the following information: ✚ E5—indicating the grid square of the map in which the Wallace Collection will be found.

The city-center maps found on the inside front and back covers of the book itself are for quick reference. They show the top 25 sights, described on pages 24–48, which are clearly plotted by number (**❶** – **❷❺**, not page number) from west to east across the city.

LONDON
life

INTRODUCING LONDON

Some people claim they know London. They cannot possibly. The joy of this city is that it can never be known. You could live here for 20 years or more and still be a beginner.

The stimulus of London is that there is always somewhere left to explore, something new to learn, some dynamic change afoot. Just when you think you have got to grips with it, the great city surprises and confronts you, turning all assumptions upside down. A new building will change a view, such as the one across the river from Greenwich after the arrival of the shining shaft of Canary Wharf Tower. Familiar pictures disappear at the annual rehang in the Tate Gallery, for example, and new canvases will come into view. Whole areas will change their mood, as Bankside has done, now revived as a lively strip of Thameside theaters, museum, and restaurants.

London is a fast city. It buzzes by day and night. Londoners tend to be busy, in a rush, independent. What for them is the enjoyable anonymity of a city can be tough for visitors to deal with, particularly since the climate does not encourage a café society for much of the year. But take a deep breath and join in London life at London's pace, and you will be swept up into the day-long feasts of London's treats.

Canary Wharf and
Canary Wharf Tower,
Docklands

London can be an expensive city. But Londoners know how to get the most out of it—from the parks, the free great national museums, the churches with free music, and traditional events with their parades and colors, to travelcards,

special theater deals, and much, much more. London on a budget need not restrict you.

London is in an administrative muddle. For a city that was once the powerful capital of an efficiently run empire stretching around the world, London today is in an astounding mess. It has no central city administration, no properly co-ordinated public transportation, and too many cars. And yet London has its own order. This city is rare in being truly cosmopolitan and the political, economic, and cultural capital of the country. Its citizens share the rhythm of the seasons in the great parks. They share in the annual round of tradition and culture such as walking in St. James's Park at daffodil time, lining up for bargain concert tickets at the Proms, and checking out London changes, be it the giant Dome or new Tate Gallery of Modern Art.

It is this rich mixture of continuity and dynamism that makes London unique and special.

A floodlit Tower Bridge silhouettes the Waterfall *sculpture in Tower Bridge Piazza*

The Thames

"The old river on its broad reach unrolled at the decline of day, after ages of good service done to the race that people its bank, spread out in the tranquil dignity of a waterway leading to the uttermost ends of the earth… What greatness had not floated on the ebb of that river into the mystery of an unknown earth… the dreams of men, the seed of commonwealth, the germs of empires."

Joseph Conrad, *Heart of Darkness*

LONDON IN FIGURES

City site
- The capital of England and Great Britain was founded by the Romans in AD 43 as a trading port on the River Thames, 40 miles inland from the North Sea.

- London is really two cities. The City of London has its origins in the Roman port and is still the commercial center. The City of Westminster, founded a thousand years later 2½ miles upstream, has always been the royal, political, and religious center.

Green places
- Greater London covers 625 square miles, of which 11 percent comprises 1,700 parks.

Languages & nationalities
- Almost 200 languages are spoken in London. About 30 percent of Londoners were born elsewhere. English is the predominant language, followed by Bengali and then Turkish, the Chinese languages, Gujarati, Urdu, Punjabi, Arabic, and Spanish.

Economy
- London's principal industries are retailing, the public sector, and tourism, followed by banking, insurance, transportation, communications, and manufacturing.

Tourists
- There are 29 million overseas and British visitors to London a year.

- The top attractions are the British Museum, the National Gallery, Madame Tussaud's, the Tower of London, and the Tate Gallery.

Population
- During the 16th century, London was Europe's fastest-growing city; its population rose from 75,000 to 200,000.

- By 1700, London was Europe's biggest and wealthiest city, with about 700,000 people.

- London continued to grow, from under 1 million in 1800 to 6.5 million by 1900, peaking in the 1930s and 1940s at 10 million.

- The population is now 7 million but rising.

LONDON PEOPLE

SIR TERENCE CONRAN
Synonymous with the shopping revolution of the 1970s, when he founded the Habitat furniture chain (► 75), Conran remains a pioneer. His Conran stores sell good design at affordable prices. The heart of Conran's empire is Butler's Wharf, where the Blue Print café sits above his Design Museum, near three of his many restaurants.

DAMIEN HIRST
Born in Bristol in 1965, this *enfant terrible* of contemporary art studied at London's Goldsmiths College before exhibiting in the landmark "Freeze" exhibition in the Docklands in 1988. A member of the "young British artist" (yBa), Hirst explores mortality in his best-known, witty series—dead animals presented in tanks or sliced up. See his works in the Tate Gallery.

RICHARD ROGERS
The architect and vision behind the Millennium Experience, Greenwich Peninsula, and the Royal Docks revival was born in Florence, Italy, in 1933. Having studied at London's Architectural Association, he won the RIBA Gold Medal in 1985 and was made a life peer in 1966—he rarely uses his title, Lord Rogers of Riverside. His wife Ruth created the immensely successful River Café (► 66).

BARBARA WINDSOR
The much-loved actress was born in north London to a dressmaker and a bus driver. Babs, as she was known, loved singing and dancing as child and went on the stage aged 12. Her role as the glamorous dolly bird in the "Carry On" films brought her fame; more recently she has appeared in the soap opera, *East Enders*, as well as seasonal theater shows.

VIVIENNE WESTWOOD
Britain's brightest and wackiest clothes designer maintains a prominent place in the fashion avant-garde. While in the King's Road, she created punk street style, but after fashion shows such as "Witches and Hypnos" she moved upscale to Mayfair where she is just as crazily imaginative.

The Governor of H.M. The Tower of London
The Governor of H.M. The Tower of London lives in a house on Tower Green and is in local command of the Tower and its 150 or so residents. The current Governor, Major-General Geoffrey Field, is not only responsible for the Crown Jewels and running the Tower; he is actively committed to revitalizing the surrounding area and may well realize his dream of flooding the Tower's moat.

Bold and beautiful: Vivienne Westwood

A Chronology

AD 43	Emperor Claudius invades Britain; a deep-water port, Londinium, is soon established.
200	The Romans put a wall around Londinium, now capital of Britannia Superior; they withdraw in 410.
1042	Edward the Confessor becomes king making London capital of England and Westminster his home; begins the abbey church of St. Peter.
1066	The Norman king, William the Conqueror, defeats King Harold at the Battle of Hastings; begins the Tower of London.
1176	Peter de Colechurch builds London's first stone bridge—London Bridge.
1477	William Caxton publishes the first book printed in England on his letter presses at Westminster.
1485	Tudor rule begins, ending 1603. London is Europe's fastest-growing city.
1529	Cardinal Thomas Wolsey fails to win Henry VIII a divorce and falls from favor.
1531	Inigo Jones designs London's first square, Covent Garden Piazza.
1533	Henry VIII breaks with Rome to marry Anne Boleyn; establishes the Church of England.
1649	Charles I is executed in Whitehall; the Commonwealth (1649–53) and Protectorate (1653–9) govern England until Charles II is restored to the throne in 1660.
1666	The Great Fire of London. Sir Christopher Wren begins St. Paul's Cathedral in 1675.
1694	William Paterson founds the Bank of England to fund William and Mary's war with France.
1759	The British Museum, London's first public museum, opens.

1800–1900	London's population grows from 1 million to 6.5 million; 14 Thames bridges are built 1811–17 and 15 railroad stations 1836–74.
1802	London becomes the world's largest port.
1816–28	John Nash lays out Regent Street, Regent's Park, and Regent's Canal.
1834	The Palace of Westminster burns down; the new building is almost complete by 1858.
1837	Queen Victoria begins her 64-year reign.
1851	The Great Exhibition is held in Hyde Park.
1863	World's first urban underground train service opens. In 1890 the first tube train runs.
1922	First daily wireless (radio) program broadcast from Savoy Hill; BBC, established 1927, first broadcasts in 1936 from Alexandra Palace.
1939–45	Blitz bombings destroy a third of the City of London and much of the docks.
1951	Festival of Britain held on the site of the South Bank arts complex.
1960s	The Beatles, Carnaby Street, and the King's Road help create "swinging London".
1980s	Post-war conservation movements save 30,000 London buildings from demolition.
1981	Revival of Docklands begins.
1994	First Eurostar trains travel through the Channel Tunnel between London and Paris.
2000	Millennium projects include the Millennium Experience, Millennium Bridge, rebuilding Sadler's Wells and Royal Opera House theaters, creating the Tate Gallery of Modern Art and Museum in Docklands, and major projects at the British, Science, and Imperial War museums.

PEOPLE & EVENTS FROM HISTORY

QUEEN BOUDICCA

In AD 62, when the widowed Boudicca, Queen of the Iceni in Norfolk, found herself insulted,

Statue of Boudicca on Westminster Bridge

dispossessed, and flogged by the Roman Procurator, she and her people revolted. They sacked Colchester, then marched on to London while its governor was away. The thriving city was plundered and laid to waste. In 1902 Thomas Thorneycroft immortalized the heroine Queen and her daughters in his bronze on Westminster Bridge.

SIR HUGH MYDDELTON

The statue of a Tudor aristocrat in doublet and hose stands on Islington Green. This is Sir Hugh Myddelton, a wealthy Welsh goldsmith who became jeweler to James I. Recognizing the lack of good clean water in the city, he cut a channel from the River Lea, 40 miles away in Hertfordshire, to bring fresh water directly into London—for which he was rewarded with a baronetcy.

JOHN NASH

John Nash created theatrical, stucco-fronted architectural designs. From 1811 onwards, backed by the Prince Regent (later George IV), he gave London its first large-scale unified plan. The great sweep of Regent Street from St. James's Park through Portland Place to Regent's Park emulated Paris in its order and grandeur.

SIR JOSEPH BAZALGETTE

As the population of London grew, so did the amount of sewage pouring into the Thames, until in summer it was known as the Great Stink. Bazalgette solved the problem by building the 3½-mile Victoria Embankment (1864–74). It incorporates a trunk sewer, underground railroad and flood wall, and is topped by a road, riverside walk, and Embankment Gardens.

The Great Fire of London

The fire that broke out at a baker's near Pudding Lane on the night of September 2nd, 1666, was the worst of many fires around that time. Raging for four days and nights, it destroyed four-fifths of the City and 13,200 homes. Sir Christopher Wren, grand architect of the consequent rebuilding of London, designed St. Paul's Cathedral, 51 churches (23 still stand), and the Monument to the tragic fire.

LONDON
how to organize your time

13

Itineraries

Walking is the best way to get under London's skin. Using the map, select
an area and simply explore. Here are four ideas—but do wander off down
an alleyway or into an old shop or a church if you see something intriguing.

ITINERARY ONE	**EARLY LONDON: THE CITY**
	It is best to walk around the City on a weekday.
Breakfast	Hearty breakfast at a Smithfield pub.
Morning	St. Bartholomew-the-Great (➤ 46).
	Walk through the medieval side streets to the Museum of London (➤ 47).
	Roman wall in the Barbican and Noble Street.
	Goldsmith's Hall and Foster Lane.
	Walk along Cheapside, down Bow Lane, and left up Queen Victoria Street.
Lunch	Sweetings seafood restaurant (➤ 64 panel).
Afternoon	Temple of Mithras, Bucklersbury (➤ 60).
	St. Margaret, Lothbury (➤ 55).
	Guildhall: huge medieval crypt, Clockmakers' Company clocks ⊙ Mon–Fri 9:30–4:45 ⊞ Free
ITINERARY TWO	**CHIC LONDON: ST. JAMES'S**
	Especially good for art galleries; best weekdays.
Morning	Jermyn Street (➤ 70), then St. James's Square and King Street (Spinks and Christie's ➤ 73).
	St. James's Palace, where the Changing of the Guard begins (➤ 22).
	Up St. James's Street and into St. James's Place to Spencer House ⊙ Sun only. Closed Jan, Aug ⊞ Moderate
	Through the tunnel to Queen's Walk by Green Park (➤ 56). Stop for a picnic lunch or:
Lunch	Café Torino ✉ 189 Piccadilly
Afternoon	Walk along Piccadilly, delving into the Ritz, Fortnum & Mason, and Hatchards (➤ 74).
	St. James's Church (➤ 55).
	The Royal Academy (➤ 51).
	Through Burlington Arcade to Cork Street art galleries (➤ 73 Waddington Galleries).
	Bond Street, New and Old (➤ 70); Sotheby's (➤ 73).

ITINERARY THREE	**ROYAL LONDON**
	Choose a dry day on which to alternate parks and picnics with palaces and palatial houses.
Morning	Kensington Palace and Kensington Gardens (➤ 25). Hyde Park (➤ 56). Apsley House (➤ 52). Green Park (➤ 56). Buckingham Palace (the Queen's Gallery is the part most likely to be open ➤ 32).
Lunch	Picnic lunch in St. James's Park (➤ 33).
Afternoon	Horse Guards through to Banqueting House (➤ 37). Parliament Square, filled with statues of past prime ministers. The Houses of Parliament (➤ 36). Westminster Abbey, where there may be afternoon evensong (➤ 35).
ITINERARY FOUR	**LONDON, CAPITAL OF AN EMPIRE**
	You will need to use some public transportation on this walk.
Morning	St. Paul's Cathedral (➤ 45): public statues and memorials in St. Paul's, and the streets around. Take bus No. 11, 15, or 23 to Trafalgar Square, dedicated to Nelson and sea heroes (➤ 53). National Portrait Gallery (➤ 38). Walk towards Buckingham Palace, up The Mall, laid out as a processional route for Queen Victoria. There's a triumphal arch at one end and her memorial at the other, set in a circle symbolizing the Empress at the heart of her empire.
Lunch	Dip into St. James's Park for lunch (➤ 33).
Afternoon	Take the underground (District or Circle line) from St. James's Park to High Street Kensington or the No. 9 bus from Trafalgar Square via Hyde Park Corner to Kensington High Street. Pay a visit to the museum in artist Linley Sambourne's former home at 8 Stafford Terrace, or to Leighton House (➤ 52).

15

WALKS

THE SIGHTS

- Tower Bridge Museum
  (► 57)
- Design Museum (► 50)
- Bramah Tea and Coffee
  Museum, Clove Building,
  Maguire Street
  ☎ 020 7378 0222
- H.M.S. *Belfast* (► 58)
- The London Dungeon,
  28–34 Tooley Street
  ☎ 020 7403 7221
  🕐 Daily 10:30–5
- International Shakespeare
  Globe Centre, New Globe
  Walk, Bankside, SE1
  ☎ 020 7902 1500
  🕐 Daily 10–5
- The Tate Gallery of Modern
  Art (► 34 and 54)
- South Bank arts complex
  (► 80)
- London Aquarium (► 51)

INFORMATION

Distance Approx 1½ miles
Time 2–3 hours, depending on
  indoor visits
Start point Tower Bridge
  ➕ K6
  🚇 Tower Hill
End point Royal Festival Hall,
  South Bank
  ➕ G6
  🚇 Waterloo, Embankment
  🚆 Waterloo

THE SOUTH BANK: THE DESIGN MUSEUM TO WESTMINSTER BRIDGE

This walk hugs the bank of the Thames and enjoys superb views across London's core on the north bank. Begin at Tower Bridge Museum, for high-level London views. Then stroll eastward among the old warehouses and new restaurants of Shad Thames to find Anthony Donaldson's *Waterfall* sculpture in Tower Bridge Piazza, Piers Gough's dramatic *The Circle*, the riverfront Design Museum on Butler's Wharf, and the Bramah Tea and Coffee Museum behind.

West of Tower Bridge, the path leads to H.M.S. *Belfast* and Hay's Galleria for more cafés. The London Dungeon lies behind. Outside the Cottons Centre is a pavilion where a map plots the buildings along the City view. Over London Bridge and past Vinopolis wine experience, take in Southwark Cathedral, and a wall and rose window of the 14th-century Winchester Palace's Great Hall.

Between Southwark and Blackfriars bridges is the Shakespeare's Globe theater, the Tate Gallery of Modern Art, and the Oxo Tower. The riverfront widens at the South Bank arts complex; beyond lies the London Aquarium. Hungerford footbridge leads to Charing Cross, Westminster Bridge to Westminster.

Monument (1408) to poet John Gower, Southwark Cathedral

16

THE TWO CITIES: CITY OF WESTMINSTER TO THE CITY OF LONDON

The heart of Westminster is still Westminster Abbey and the Houses of Parliament—there is a good view of the riverfront from the south end of Westminster Bridge.

From statue-filled Parliament Square (there is a diagram of who's who on the east side), Whitehall leads up past Downing Street—official residence of the Prime Minister—Horse Guards, and Banqueting House, to Trafalgar Square, home of the National Gallery. The National Portrait Gallery is at the end of St. Martin's Lane. Farther on, past the Coliseum, turn right through New Row into Covent Garden, a good place to stop for refreshment. On the piazza, find the London Transport Museum and nearby, the Theatre Museum. Down on the Strand, turn left and go through Aldwych to the Courtauld Gallery on the south side.

In Fleet Street, winged dragons mark the boundary of the City of London and Westminster. Just before Chancery Lane, an alley on the right leads to Temple Church and the Inner and Middle Inns. Farther on, Johnson's Court, on the left (between Nos. 166 and 167), leads to Dr. Johnson's House, while St. Bride's is on the right, tucked behind the Reuters building. St. Paul's Cathedral stands at the top of Ludgate Hill. Behind it, Watling Street leads to Bow Lane and a choice of places for lunch or dinner.

THE SIGHTS

- Westminster Bridge
- Houses of Parliament (➤ 36)
- Westminster Abbey (➤ 35)
- Parliament Square
- Whitehall
- Downing Street
- Horse Guards
- Banqueting House (➤ 37)
- National Gallery (➤ 39)
- National Portrait Gallery (➤ 38)
- Coliseum (➤ 80)
- Covent Garden (➤ 40)
- London Transport Museum (➤ 40)
- Strand
- Courtauld Gallery (➤ 41)
- Fleet Street
- Temple Church (➤ 55)
- Inns of Court, Inner and Middle Temple (➤ 60)
- Dr. Johnson's House (➤ 52)
- St. Bride's Church
- St. Paul's Cathedral (➤ 45)
- Bow Lane

INFORMATION

Distance 2–2½ miles
Time 3–6 hours, depending on museum and church visits
Start point Westminster Bridge
🚇 G6
🚉 Westminster
End point Bow Street
🚇 G5
🚉 Mansion House

Statue of 2nd Duke of Cambridge (1819–1904), by Adrian Jones, in Whitehall 17

EVENING STROLLS

London is gently lit by streetlights, neon signs and the occasional floodlight, nothing very dramatic. Look for the surviving gas lamps. Both of the following strolls end in Soho, the heart of nighttime London.

INFORMATION

**Royal & Aristocratic
Evocations**
Distance ½ mile
Time 30–40 minutes
Start point Buckingham Palace
➕ F6
🚇 Green Park, St. James's Park
   or Victoria
End point Piccadilly Circus
➕ F5
🚇 Piccadilly Circus

The Political Path
Distance ½ mile
Time 40 minutes–1 hour
Start point Westminster Bridge
➕ G6
🚇 Westminster
End point Shaftesbury Avenue
➕ F5–G5
🚇 Piccadilly Circus or
   Leicester Square

ROYAL & ARISTOCRATIC EVOCATIONS

Buckingham Palace's gray Portland stone has a more fairy-tale quality at night. In front of it glints the Queen Victoria Memorial, while St. James's Park's fountains sparkle under floodlights.

Marlborough Road leads from The Mall to Pall Mall, where gas flares may illuminate an old club's facade. The redbrick of St. James's Palace glows warmly, and old gas lamps shed a gentle light on the lanes behind it and to the left up St. James's Street. Along Piccadilly, Piccadilly Circus's neon lights and Eros statue are the gateway to Shaftesbury Avenue's theaters and Soho's nightlife.

THE POLITICAL PATH

From Westminster Bridge, enjoy close-ups of the Houses of Parliament and gilded Big Ben, and distant views along the twisting Thames to St. Paul's Cathedral and the City. In Parliament Square and up Whitehall, spot who was who in the statues of London's heroes and villains.

Lutyens's fountains splash at the foot of Nelson's illuminated column in Trafalgar Square; other naval stars surround him. Up behind the National Gallery, Leicester Square's great movie theaters dwarf the crowds of visitors and the occasional street musician. Chinese Soho, perfumed by its many fine restaurants, fills the lanes north of here to Shaftesbury Avenue, the focus being pedestrianized Gerrard Street.

ORGANIZED SIGHTSEEING

Taking a guided tour is a good way to enjoy a London panorama and gain in-depth information from a Londoner. Walking tours get deeper into London life. They have good leaders, are low-cost, and do not need reserving in advance. Bus tours have various pick-up points, including some hotels. See also the Thames (► 57), National Theatre (► 79), and Dickens House (► 44). For a tailor-made tour with a Blue Badge trained guide (a rigorous qualification) ✉ 020 7495 5504

THE BIG BUS COMPANY
Live commentary on double-decker buses; Panoramic and Stopper tours (hop-on hop-off). ✉ Waterside Way, SW17 ☎ 020 8944 7810

BUS TRIP TO MURDER
The "hit list" includes Jack the Ripper on this 3½-hour evening tour. Reservations are a must. ✉ Tragical History Tours ☎ 020 8857 1545 🕐 Tue, Thu–Sun

EVAN EVANS
Blue Badge guides for walks (for example, Jack the Ripper), river cruises, and out-of-town tours. ✉ 26 Cockspur Street, Trafalgar Square, SW1 ☎ 020 8332 2222

FRAMES RICKARDS
Blue Badge guides for general, evening, thematic (ghosts, for example), and out-of-town tours. ✉ 11 Herbrand Street, WC1 ☎ 020 7837 3111

THE ORIGINAL LONDON SIGHTSEEING TOUR
Taped or live commentary (eight languages) on four interconnecting tours (► 59 for the tour); live commentary for "London Plus" tours. ✉ London Coaches, Jews Road, SW18 ☎ 020 8877 1722

THE ORIGINAL LONDON WALKS
The Tuckers organize a walk for most days of the year, guided by enthusiasts and experts. ✉ P.O. Box 1708, NW6 ☎ 020 7624 3978

TAKE-A-GUIDE
Tailor-made tours by foot or car. ✉ 43 Finstock Road, W10 ☎ 020 8960 0459

Buildings and more buildings

Various societies organize tours to look at London's architecture. Architectural Dialogue (☎ 020 8341 1371) have Saturday morning and other tours led by architects and architectural historians. The Georgian Group (☎ 020 7387 1720), Victorian Society (☎ 020 8994 1019), and Twentieth Century Society (☎ 020 7250 3857) all do walks and tours, too.

EXCURSIONS

INFORMATION

Greenwich

Distance 4 miles from London
Bridge and Tower Hill, 5
miles from Westminster
Bridge

Journey time 20 minutes–1 hour

🚊 Docklands Light Railway to
Island Gardens, then foot
tunnel

🚢 Riverboat from Westminster
and other piers

ℹ️ 46 Greenwich Church Street,
SE10 ☎ 020 8858 6376
🕐 Daily 10:15–4:45

National Maritime Museum

✉️ Romney Road, SE10

☎ 020 8858 4422

🕐 Daily 10–5

🎫 Very expensive

Hampton Court

Distance Approx. 11 miles

Journey time 30 minutes by
train, 3–4 hours by boat

🚊 Waterloo railroad station to
Hampton Court

🚢 Riverboat from Westminster
Pier

Hampton Court Palace

✉️ East Molesey, Surrey

☎ 020 8781 9500

🕐 Summer: Tue–Sun 9:30–6;
Mon 10:15–6. Winter:
Tue–Sun 9:30–4:30;
Mon 10:15–4:30

🎫 Very expensive

GREENWICH

Downstream from the City lies Greenwich. At
its core is a favorite royal palace, the Queen's
House, designed by Inigo Jones, which is
surrounded by the Royal Naval College
(formerly the Royal Naval Hospital), designed
by Christopher Wren. Go early and for the
whole day. There is plenty to see, plus markets
and craft fairs on the weekends (► 72).

The National Maritime Museum, the world's
largest nautical museum, fills the old Royal
Hospital School and incorporates Queen's
House. Up the hill is the Royal Observatory,
Greenwich—the Greenwich Meridian (0° longi-
tude) passes through here. Nearby, the hilltop
row houses provides London's grandest view;
behind lie the Ranger's House and the Fan
Museum. Before you leave, see the Painted Hall
and Chapel inside Wren's Hospital, and two special boats: the *Cutty Sark* and *Gipsy Moth IV.*

HAMPTON COURT PALACE

This is London's most impressive royal palace,
well worth the journey west out of the city center.
When King Henry VIII dismissed Cardinal
Wolsey in 1529, he took over his already
ostentatious Tudor palace and enlarged it.
Successive monarchs altered and repaired both
the palace and its 60 acres of Tudor and baroque
gardens.

The best way to visit this huge collection of
chambers, courtyards, and state apartments is to
follow one of the six clearly indicated routes—
perhaps Henry VIII's State Apartments or
the King's Apartments built for William III,
immaculately restored after a devastating fire.
Outside, do not miss the Tudor gardens, the
Maze, and restored Privy Garden, where there
are guided historical walks each afternoon.

WINDSOR

The fairy-tale towers and turrets of Windsor
Castle make this the ultimate queen's castle—it
is indeed an official residence of the Queen and

her court. Begun by William the Conqueror, rebuilt in stone by Henry II, there have been embellishments ever since. Various parts are open; if the State Apartments and St. George's Chapel are closed, there is still plenty to see. Changing of the Guard is at 11AM.

Outside the castle lie Windsor's pretty, medieval cobblestone lanes, Christopher Wren's Guildhall, and the delightful Theatre Royal. Beyond it, you can explore Windsor Great Park's 4,800 acres with their stunning views, or cross the Thames to Eton.

A ROBERT ADAM DOUBLE: SYON & OSTERLEY

To use public transportation and see both houses, do this trip on a Saturday.

Two magnificent country mansions and their parks lie southwest of London. At each, with meticulous attention to detail both inside and out, Robert Adam transformed a 16th-century house into an elegant neoclassical mansion.

Osterley is a rare example of a well-preserved house and 140-acre park close to London. First completed in 1575, Adam's transformation in 1760–80 was for the banker Robert Child. Thameside Syon is even more sumptuous. Its opulent furnishings were made for Hugh Smithson, 1st Duke of Northumberland, whose family still owns Syon. Don't miss the Conservatory or London Butterfly House.

Syon House

INFORMATION

Windsor
Distance 17 miles
Journey time 35–50 minutes
📺 Waterloo or Paddington
🚌 24 High Street ☎ 01753
743900 🕐 Mon–Sat
9:30–5; Sun 10–5

Windsor Castle
☎ 01753 868286
🕐 Mar–Oct: daily 10–5.
Nov–Feb: daily 10–3
💷 Very expensive

Syon & Osterley
Distance 9 miles
Journey time 1 hour to either
📺 Osterley; then bus H28, H91
to Syon. From Syon bus
237, 267 to Kew Bridge for
Waterloo.

Syon House
✉ Brentford, Middlesex
☎ 020 8560 0883
🕐 House Mar–Oct: Wed–Sun;
bank holidays 11–5.
Park daily 10–6 or dusk.
London Butterfly House
daily 10–3:30
💷 Expensive

Osterley Park
✉ Isleworth, Middlesex
☎ 020 8568 7714
🕐 House Apr–Oct: Wed–Sun
1–4:30. Closed Good Fri.
Park 9–7:30 or dusk
💷 Moderate

21

WHAT'S ON

London's festivals and traditions provide free, colorful events and are often the chance to see buildings usually closed to the public. The London Tourist Board publishes a free festivals booklet; most are also in the weekly listings in the magazine *Time Out*.

January	*The sales* (most of Jan): Shopping bargains.
February	*Chinese New Year* (end of Feb): Dragon dances and fireworks in Soho.
March	*Chelsea Antiques Fair*: Chelsea Old Town Hall.
April	*Oxford and Cambridge Boat Race* (1st Saturday): Putney to Mortlake on the Thames.
	London Marathon (1st Sunday).
May	*Chelsea Flower Show* (end of May): One of the world's best, at the Royal Hospital, Chelsea.
June	*Trooping the Colour* (2nd Saturday): The "Colours" (flags) are trooped before the Queen on Horseguards Parade, Whitehall.
	Wimbledon (end of Jun): The world's leading tennis tournament.
July	*Promenade Concerts—"The Proms"* (Jul and Aug): A series of classical concerts in the Albert Hall.
August	*Notting Hill Carnival* (last weekend, Bank Holiday Monday): Europe's biggest.
September	*Election of the Lord Mayor of London* (Sep 29): The Lord Mayor and his successor-elect ride in the state coach to the Mansion House.
October	(1st Sunday): "Pearly Kings and Queens" service at St. Martin-in-the-Fields.
November	*Bonfire Night* (Nov 5): Fires and fireworks commemorate the failed "Gunpowder Plot" of 1605.
	State Opening of Parliament: Royal procession from Buckingham Palace to Houses of Parliament.
December	*Christmas Tree* (mid-month): The annual gift from Norway is raised in Trafalgar Square.
Daily	*The Changing of the Guard*: At St. James's Palace, Guards march to Buckingham Palace at 11:15, returning at 12:10; at Buckingham Palace, the Guard is changed at 11:30 daily Apr–Aug 7, otherwise alternate days; at Horse Guards, by the former Whitehall Palace, at 11 daily, Sun at 10; at Windsor Castle, at 11 on alternate weekdays in winter, daily in summer (except Sun). Ceremonies are canceled in very bad weather. ☎ 0839 123411 for current information.

LONDON's
top 25 sights

The sights are shown on the maps on the inside front cover and inside back cover, numbered **1–25** *from west to east across the city*

ROYAL BOTANICAL GARDENS, KEW

HIGHLIGHTS

- Arriving by riverboat
- Japanese Gateway
- Gallery walks, Palm House
- Temperate House
- Springtime woods and dells
- Oak Avenue to Queen Charlotte's Cottage

INFORMATION

✉ Kew Road, Kew, Richmond
☎ 020 8940 1171
🕐 Daily from 9:30AM. Closing time varies. Closed Dec 25, Jan 1
🍴 Good
🔲 Kew Gardens
🚊 Kew Bridge
♿ Excellent
Ⓜ Moderate
↔ Syon House (► 21)
❓ Guided tours 11, 2; jazz concerts 3rd week in Jul; orchid show Feb–Mar

The Princess of Wales Conservatory

24

Whether the trees are shrouded in winter mists, the azaleas are bursting with blossoms, or the lawns are dotted with summer picnickers reading Sunday newspapers, Kew Gardens never fail to work their magic.

Royal beginnings The 300-acre gardens, containing 44,000 different plants and many glorious greenhouses, make up the world's foremost botanical research center. But it began modestly. George III's mother, Princess Augusta, planted 9 acres around tiny Kew Palace in 1759, helped by gardener William Aiton and botanist Lord Bute. Architect Sir William Chambers built the Pagoda, Orangery, Ruined Arch, and three temples. Later, George III enlarged the gardens to their present size and Sir Joseph Banks (head gardener 1772–1819), who had traveled with Captain Cook, planted them with specimens from all over the world.

Victorian order When the gardens were given to the nation in 1841, Sir William Hooker became director for 24 years. He founded the Department of Economic Botany, the museums, the Herbarium, and the Library, while W. A. Nesfield laid out the lake, pond, and the four great vistas: Pagoda Vista, Broad Walk, Holly Walk, and Cedar Vista.

The greenhouses Chambers' Orangery is now the Gardens' shop and restaurant. To see plant-filled greenhouses, seek out Decimus Burton's stunning Palm House (1844–8), his Temperate House (1860–2, when it was the world's largest greenhouse), Waterlily House (1852), and the Princess of Wales Conservatory (1987). The 1990s exhibition, Evolution, is in the 1950s Australia House.

2

KENSINGTON PALACE & GARDENS

It gives King William III a human dimension that he suffered from asthma, a modern complaint, and so moved out of dank Whitehall Palace to a mansion in the clean air of tiny Kensington village. This royal home retains a domestic feel.

The perfect location The year he became king, 1689, William and his wife Mary bought their mansion, perfectly positioned for London socializing and country living. They brought in Sir Christopher Wren and Nicholas Hawksmoor to remodel and enlarge the house, and moved in for Christmas.

A favorite royal home Despite the small rooms, George I introduced palatial grandeur with Colen Campbell's staircase and state rooms, elegantly decorated by William Kent. Meanwhile, Queen Anne added the Orangery (the architect was Hawksmoor, the woodcarver Grinling Gibbons) and annexed a chunk of royal Hyde Park, a trick repeated by George II's wife, Queen Caroline, who created the Round Pond and Long Water to complete the 275-acre Kensington Gardens. Today, a wide variety of trees are the backdrop for sculptures by G. F. Watts, Henry Moore, and George Frampton, whose image of the fairytale Peter Pan is near the Long Water.

A very special childhood On May 24, 1819, Queen Victoria was born here. She was baptized in the splendid Cupola Room, spent her childhood in rooms overlooking the gardens (now filled with Victoria memorabilia) and, on June 20, 1837, learned here she was to be queen. After moving into Buckingham Palace, she opened to the public the State Apartments and gardens of her childhood home.

HIGHLIGHTS

- King's Grand Staircase
- Presence Chamber
- Wind dial in the King's Gallery
- King's Drawing Room
- Princess Victoria's dolls' house
- Round Pond
- Summer tea in the Orangery
- Walks
- Serpentine Gallery
- Italian Gardens

INFORMATION

- C6
- Kensington Gardens, W8
- 020 7937 9561
- Daily 10–5. Oct–Apr: Wed–Sun 10–4. Closed Dec 24–26, Jan 1, Good Fri
- Café in palace (winter) or Orangery (summer)
- High Street Kensington or Queensway
- Few
- Expensive; family tickets
- Natural History Museum (➤ 26), Science Museum (➤ 27), V&A Museum (➤ 28)
- Guided tour every 30 minutes

25

3

NATURAL HISTORY MUSEUM

INFORMATION

- ✚ C7
- ✉ Cromwell Road, SW7; also entrance on Exhibition Road
- ☎ 020 7938 9123
- 🕐 Mon–Sat 10–5:50; Sun 11–5:50. Closed Dec 23–26
- 🍴 Meals, snacks, picnic areas
- Ⓢ South Kensington
- ♿ Excellent
- 💷 Expensive. Free after 4:30 Mon–Fri, after 5 Sat, Sun. South Kensington Museums season ticket applies
- ↔ Kensington Palace (➤ 25), Science Museum (➤ 27), V&A Museum (➤ 28)
- ❓ Regular tours, lectures, films, workshops

Top: the entrance hall
Below: the East Wing

Before you go in, look at the museum building. It looks like a striped, Romanesque cathedral and is wittily decorated with a zoo of animals to match its contents: extant animals on the west side, extinct ones on the east side.

Two museums in one Overflowing the British Museum where they were originally housed, the Life Galleries were moved to Alfred Waterhouse's honey-and-blue-striped building in 1880. They tell the story of life on earth. The Earth Galleries tell the story of the earth itself, beginning with a 300-million-year-old fossil of a fern.

Dinosaurs in the Life Galleries The nave of Waterhouse's cathedral contains a plaster cast of the vast skeleton of the 150-million-year-old diplodocus (the original is in Pittsburgh, Pennsylvania). In the surrounding bays are fore-tastes of discoveries to be made in the galleries: a pygmy chimpanzee skeleton, huge deer antlers 11,000 years old, and much more. The lively exhibition galleries focus on the relevance of the dinosaur world, the human body, mammals, birds, the marine world today, and "creepy crawlies" (the 800,000 known species of insect are added to every year)—all with plenty of slides, models, and hands-on games.

The Earth Galleries These offer a fascinating exploration of our planet. The Earthquake Experience is set in a Japanese supermarket, the Restless Surface explores the effects of natural forces on the earth, and the Earth's Treasury looks at the gemstones and minerals lying beneath the earth's crust.

SCIENCE MUSEUM

Even if you are no scientist, it's thrilling to understand how a plane flies, how Newton's reflecting telescope worked, or how we receive satellite television. This is science made fun.

Industry and science Opened in 1857 and once part of the Victoria & Albert Museum, this is the museum that comes closest to fulfilling Prince Albert's educational aims when he founded the South Kensington Museums after the Great Exhibition of 1851. Its full title is the National Museum of Science and Industry. Therefore, over the five floors, which contain more than 60 collections, the story of human industry, discovery, and invention is recounted through various tools and products, from exquisite Georgian cabinets to a satellite launcher.

Science made fun People walk, talk, laugh, and get excited by what they see here. Visitors of all ages are interested to see how vital every day objects were invented and then developed for use. The spinning wheel, steam engine, car, and television have changed our lives. The industrial society in which we live could not do without plastic, but how is it made?

All kinds of science The galleries vary from rooms of beautiful 18th-century objects to in-depth explanations of abstract concepts: You can use the hands-on equipment in Flight Lab to learn the basic principles of flying. The Wellcome Museum of the History of Medicine, on the topmost floors, includes an exhibit on prehistoric bone surgery and an X-ray room. The Challenge of Materials and The Science of Sport are new galleries; meanwhile, a whole new Wellcome Wing exploring science and medicine opens in 2000.

HIGHLIGHTS

- Demonstrations
- Taking part in Launch Pad
- The hands-on basement area
- Flight Lab
- Apollo 10 module
- Puffing Billy
- Amy Johnson's aeroplane, *Jason*
- 18th-century watches and clocks
- The Science of Sport
- Historical characters explaining their achievements

INFORMATION

- ✚ C7
- ✉ Exhibition Road, SW7
- ☎ 020 7938 8000
- 🕐 Daily 10–6. Closed Dec 24–26
- 🍴 Café, picnic area
- 🚇 South Kensington
- ♿ Excellent, plus helpline ☎ 020 7938 9788
- 💷 Expensive. Free after 4:30. Family and season tickets. South Kensington Museums season ticket applies
- ❓ Guided tours, demonstrations, historic characters, lectures, films, workshops
- ↔ Natural History Museum (▶ 26)

Top: Apollo 10 module in the Exploration of Space Gallery

5

VICTORIA & ALBERT MUSEUM

HIGHLIGHTS

- Medieval ivory carvings
- Jones porcelain collection
- Glass Gallery
- Shah Jahan's Jade Cup
- Canning Jewel
- New Raphael Gallery
- Frank Lloyd Wright Room
- Silver galleries

INFORMATION

- ✚ D7
- ✉ Cromwell Road, SW7
- ☎ 020 7938 8500
- 🕐 Daily 10–4:45. Seasonal late openings. Closed Dec 24–26, Jan 1, Good Fri, May Day
- 🍴 Basement restaurant, café
- Ⓢ South Kensington
- ♿ Very good
- 💷 Expensive. South Kensington Museums ticket applies
- ↔ Natural History Museum (➤ 26), Science Museum (➤ 27)
- ❓ Guided tours, talks, courses, concerts

Detail, facade

Part of the Victoria & Albert Museum's glory is that each room is unexpected; it may contain a French boudoir, plaster casts of classical sculptures, or exquisite contemporary glass, diverting you so happily that sometimes you will never reach your original goal.

An optimistic foundation The V&A, as it is fondly known, started as the South Kensington Museum. It was Prince Albert's vision: arts and science objects available to all people to inspire them to invent and create, with the accent on commercial design and craftsmanship. Since it opened in 1857, its collection has become so encyclopedic and international that today, it is the world's largest decorative arts museum.

Bigger and bigger Its size is unmanageable: 145 galleries cover 7 miles of gallery space on six floors. Its content is even more so: barely 5 percent of the 44,000 objects in the Indian department can be on show. Larger museum objects include whole London house facades, grand rooms, and the Raphael Cartoons. Despite this, contemporary work has always been energetically bought: More than 60 percent of furniture entering the museum is 20th century.

Riches and rags Not every object in the V&A is precious: there are everyday things, unique pieces, and opportunities to discover a fascination for a new subject—perhaps lace, ironwork, tiles, Indian paintings, or Japanese textiles. The best way to tackle the V&A is either to select a favorite piece and go headlong for it, or wander happily for an hour or so, feasting on any objects that catch your eye. Look for new projects: the British Galleries reopen in 2002, and so too might Daniel Libeskind's controversial Spiral.

KENWOOD HOUSE & HAMPSTEAD HEATH

For many north Londoners, sunny Sunday mornings on Hampstead Heath are an essential part of life: locals walk their dogs and babies, sit reading the news-papers, enjoy the fine London views, and perhaps drop into Kenwood House to see a Rembrandt or two.

Kenwood House When in 1754 William Murray, Earl of Mansfield and George III's Chief Justice, bought his country house outside pretty Hampstead village spa, he brought in London's most fashionable architect, Robert Adam, to remodel it, and employed Humphry Repton to landscape the gardens. A later owner, Edward Guinness, Earl of Iveagh, hung the walls with Rembrandts, Gainsboroughs, Vermeers, and Romneys before giving the whole package, the Iveagh Bequest, to the nation.

The people's heath When Victorian London was expanding, it was the people of Hampstead who saved their valuable, open heathland from the developers' claws. Since 1829 they have pre-served, piece by piece, a total of 825 acres of rolling woodland, open grass, and spectacular views—the walled Hill Garden was added only in 1960. It is "to be kept forever…open, unenclosed and unbuilt on."

A place of many moods The heath is full of action and color when weekend kite-flyers meet on Parliament Hill. It is a place for sports, per-haps swimming or boating in Hampstead Ponds, playing hockey on East Heath, enjoying a game of tennis, or simply taking a quiet walk. There are arts celebrations, too, the best of which are the summer lakeside concerts that Londoners listen to as they picnic on the sloping lawns in front of Kenwood House.

HIGHLIGHTS

- Azaleas in the Hill Garden
- Library in Kenwood House
- Lakeside concerts
- London view from beside Kenwood House
- Oak, beech, and sweet chestnut woods
- Parliament Hill
- Crossing the Heath from Hampstead to Highgate
- Rembrandt's *Portrait of the Artist* in Kenwood House
- Carpets of spring daffodils around Kenwood

INFORMATION

- ✉ Kenwood House, Hampstead Lane, NW3
- ☎ 020 8348 1286
- 🕐 Kenwood House Apr–Sep: daily 10–6. Oct–Mar: daily 10–4. Closed Dec 24–25. The Heath daily 8AM–dusk
- 🍴 Restaurant, café
- Ⓔ Kenwood House: Golders Green. The Heath: Hampstead, Belsize Park, Highgate or Kentish Town
- 🚌 Kenwood House: 210, 271. Parliament Hill: 214, C2, C11, C12
- 🚉 Gospel Oak, Hampstead Heath
- ♿ Good
- 🆓 Free
- ❓ Guided tours for groups, indoor and outdoor concerts

REGENT'S PARK

HIGHLIGHTS

- Queen Mary's Gardens
- Lakeside strolls
- Lolling on deckchairs by the bandstand
- Nature Study Centre
- Boating on the lake
- Nesfield's restored Avenue Gardens
- Canal boat trip from the zoo to Little Venice
- 98 species of duck
- Picnicking on the lake's north bank
- Summer barbecues and open-air theater

INFORMATION

- ✚ E3
- ✉ Marylebone Road, NW1
- ☎ 020 7486 7905
- 🕐 Daily 7AM–shortly before dusk (times are posted on information boards at each gate)
- 🍴 Restaurant, cafés
- Ⓜ Baker Street, Regent's Park, Great Portland Street, or Camden Town
- ♿ Very good
- ↔ London Zoo (► 31), Madame Tussaud's Waxworks & Planetarium (► 59)
- ❓ Information boards at entrances include plans; boats for rent on the lake and children's boating pond; weekend bandstand music; open-air theater and musicals May–Sep

Regent's Park has all an urban explorer could wish for in a park: big open spaces, a lake to row on, spectacular gardens, ducks and swans in quantity, a variety of ideal picnic spots, theater and music, and free peeks at the elephants in the zoo.

The Prince's plan Regent's Park is the result of a remarkable coincidence of royal enlightenment, architectural theater, peaceful times, and a large tract of land becoming available. In 1811 the Prince Regent, later George IV, and his architect, John Nash, conceived and completed a Regency backbone for London stretching from St. James's Park up Regent Street and Portland Place to Regent's Park. After vast earth-moving activities, the park was given its undulating lawns, lake, garden, and trees, all ringed by grand row house backdrops and dotted with just eight of the 56 planned villas.

From the nobles to the people What was designed as a garden city for nobles is now the most elegant of London parks. It has been open to the public since 1835, when Regent's Canal was one of the busiest stretches of canal in Britain. Londoners flocked to visit the zoo, Inner Circle (later Queen Mary's) Gardens, and Avenue Gardens, which W. A. Nesfield designed in 1864. Its 487 acres easily absorb Muslims strolling from the gold-domed Central Mosque, patrons of the Open Air Theatre, cricketers—and many others besides.

The canal at Little Venice

LONDON ZOO

When you visit the zoo, be sure spend time looking at the wonderful gentle Asian elephants—first from Regent's Park, then inside the zoo—having a bath, throwing dust over their backs, eating, lazing about looking contented, and playing with their keeper.

Exotic animals for Londoners In 1826 Sir Stamford Raffles, who established Singapore Colony, founded the Zoological Society of London with Sir Humphry Davy. Four years later it opened 5 acres of its gardens to the public, and met with immediate success. The Society's own collection of exotic animals— zebras, monkeys, kangaroos, and bears—was soon enlarged by the royal menagerie from Windsor Castle and the royal zoo from the Tower of London.

Extraordinary animals Over the years new arrivals have included Tommy the chimpanzee in 1835 and, in 1836, the giraffes, which set a trend for giraffe-patterned fabric. Jumbo and Alice, the African elephants, were also exceedingly popular with visitors. Meanwhile, the world's first reptile house, aquarium, and insect houses were constructed.

A modern zoo Aware of the worldwide controversy over zoos, London Zoo is maintaining its place at the forefront of animal conservation and education, housing the Institute of Zoology, which carries out research, and funding fieldwork. The Children's Zoo has a "petting paddock" and a center to teach children how to care for pets. While deer roam, lions roar, and birds screech, talks, demonstrations, and the Web of Life conservation center encourage awareness of the earth's fragility.

HIGHLIGHTS

- Asian elephants
- Big cats
- Children's Zoo Pet Care Centre
- Lord Snowdon's aviaries
- Reversed lighting to see nocturnal mammals
- Feeding time for lions
- Cavorting chimpanzees
- Web of Life center
- Baby rhinos

INFORMATION

- E2 (for entrance)
- Regent's Park, NW1
- 020 7722 3333
- Apr–Oct: daily 10–5:30. Nov–Mar: daily 10–4. Closed Dec 25
- Restaurant, cafés, and kiosks
- Camden Town
- Camden Town
- Good
- Very expensive
- Regent's Park (➤ 30)
- Lectures, talks, workshops, regular animal feeding times; animal action programs daily; animal adoption schemes

Top: the elephant enclosure

31

9

BUCKINGHAM PALACE

HIGHLIGHTS

- Liveried beadles in the Queen's Gallery
- Changing of the Guard
- State Coach, Royal Mews
- Nash's facade, Quadrangle
- Gobelin tapestries in the Guard Room
- Throne Room
- Van Dyck's portrait of Charles I and family
- Table of Grand Commanders, Blue Drawing Room
- Secret royal door in the White Drawing Room
- Garden Shop

INFORMATION

- ✚ F6
- ✉ The Mall, SW1
- ☎ 020 7799 2331
- 🕐 Queen's Gallery daily 9:30–4:30 (during exhibitions).
  Royal Mews Apr–Oct: Mon–Thu noon–3:30.
  Oct–Dec: Mon, Wed noon–4. Closed Ascot week and ceremonial occasions.
  State Rooms, Buckingham Palace Aug–Sep: daily 9:30–4:30.
  Last admission at 4:30.
- 🚇 Victoria, St. James's Park, or Green Park
- 🚉 Victoria
- ♿ Excellent
- 💷 Very expensive
- ↔ Changing the Guard (➤ 22), St. James's Park (➤ 33)
- ❓ No photography

Of the London houses now open to visitors, the Queen's own home where she spends much of the year must be the most fascinating of all: Where else can you see a living sovereign's private art, drawing rooms, and horse harnesses?

Yet another palace The British sovereigns have moved around London quite a bit over the years; from Westminster to Whitehall to Kensington and St. James's, and finally to Buckingham Palace. It was George III who in 1762 bought the prime-site mansion, Buckingham House, as a gift for his new bride, the 17-year-old Queen Charlotte, leaving St. James's Palace to be the official royal residence.

Grand improvements When the Prince Regent finally became King George IV in 1820, he and his architect, John Nash, made extravagant changes using honey-colored Bath stone, all to be covered up by Edward Blore's facade added for Queen Victoria. Today, the 600 rooms and 40-acre garden include the State Apartments, offices for the Royal Household, a movie theater, swimming pool, and the Queen's private rooms overlooking Green Park.

Queen Elizabeth II opens her home The Queen inherited the world's finest private art collection. The Queen's Gallery (enlarging in time for her Golden Jubilee in 2003) exhibits some of her riches. Nearby, in the Royal Mews, Nash's stables and storerooms house gleaming fairytale coaches, harnesses, and other apparel for royal ceremonies. Make sure you do not miss the Buckingham Palace Summer Opening, when visitors can wander through the grand State Rooms, resplendent with gold, pictures, porcelain, tapestries, and of course, thrones.

St. James's Park

Even if you drop in to St. James's Park merely to eat a sandwich and laze on a deck chair while listening to the band's music, you can usually spot a trio of palaces across the duck-filled lake and over the tips of the weeping willows.

Royal through and through St. James's Park is the oldest and most thoroughly royal of London's nine royal parks, surrounded by the Palace of Westminster, St. James's Palace, Buckingham Palace, and the remains of Whitehall Palace. Kings and their courtiers have been frolicking here since Henry VIII laid out a deer park in 1532 and built a hunting lodge that became St. James's Palace. James I began the menagerie, which included pelicans, crocodiles, and an elephant who drank a gallon of wine daily.

French order Charles II, influenced by Versailles, near Paris, redesigned the park to include a canal (where he swam), Birdcage Walk (where he kept his aviaries), and the graveled Mall, where he played pell mell, a courtly French game similar to croquet. Then George IV, helped by John Nash and influenced by Humphry Repton, softened the garden's formal French lines into the English style, making this 93-acre park of blossoming shrubs and undulating, curving paths a favorite with all romantics.

Nature dominates As the park is an important migration point and breeding area for birds, two full-time ornithologists look after up to 1,000 birds from more than 45 species. Among the fig, plane, and willow trees, seek out the pelicans living on Duck Island, a tradition begun when the Russian Ambassador gave some to Charles II.

HIGHLIGHTS

- Springtime daffodils
- Whitehall from the lake bridge
- Feeding the pelicans, 3PM
- Views to Buckingham Palace
- Duck Island in springtime
- The fact that it is still not enclosed

INFORMATION

- ✚ F6
- ✉ The Mall, SW1
- ☎ 020 7930 1793
- 🕐 Daily dawn–midnight
- 🍴 Restaurant, café
- Ⓜ St. James's Park, Green Park, or Westminster
- 🚆 Victoria
- ♿ Very good
- 💷 Free
- ↔ Changing the Guard (➤ 22), Buckingham Palace (➤ 32), Banqueting House (➤ 37)
- ❓ Occasional bird talks; summer bandstand music

The Whitehall skyline seen from the park

11

TATE GALLERIES

HIGHLIGHTS

British collection
- *John, 10th Viscount Kilmorey*, Gainsborough
- *The Opening of Waterloo Bridge*, Constable
- *Interior at Petworth*, Turner

International collection
- Roomful of red Rothkos
- *The Three Dancers*, Picasso
- *The Kiss*, Rodin

INFORMATION

Tate Gallery of British Art
- ➕ G8
- ✉ Millbank, SW1
- ☎ 020 7887 8000
- ◷ Mon–Sat 10–5:50; Sun 2–5:50. Closed Dec 24–26, Jan 1, Good Fri, May Day
- 🍴 Restaurant, café
- Ⓢ Pimlico
- 🚉 Victoria
- ♿ Very good
- 🎫 Free except for special exhibitions
- ↔ Westminster Abbey (➤ 35)
- ❓ Full education program

Tate Gallery of Modern Art
- ➕ J6
- ✉ Bankside, SE1
- ☎ 020 7401 7271
- ◷ As for the Tate at Millbank
- 🍴 Restaurant, café
- Ⓢ Southwark, Blackfriars, London Bridge
- ♿ Very good
- 🎫 Free
- ❓ Full education program

The annual Tate rehangs by the director are a winter highlight: familiar pictures reappear in different places, and there are plenty of new works, both British and modern, to get to know.

Two for one The Tate, opened in 1897, is named after the sugar millionaire Henry Tate, who paid for the core building and donated his Victorian pictures to put inside it. Today, its national collections of British and international art have overflowed into a second building. The British collection remains at Millbank; the international collection fills Giles Gilbert Scott's transformed Bankside Power Station (➤ 54) across the Thames from St. Paul's Cathedral. The annual rehangs emphasize different aspects of both collections.

British art In rooms undergoing total refurbishment by 2002, you may well find the large icon-like portrait of Elizabeth I by Nicholas Hilliard and the Tate's earliest dated picture, John Bette's *Man in a Black Cap* (1545). There are portraits by Van Dyck, Hogarth, Gainsborough, and Reynolds; illustrations by Blake, landscapes by Constable, and in room 9, pictures by the Pre-Raphaelites. The Turner Collection is housed in the purpose-built Clore Gallery, designed by James Stirling.

Modern international art Pieces dating from the Impressionist period now fill the large light-drenched galleries with their spectacular city views. You may find works by Monet, Matisse, and Picasso, or by the more recent Mark Rothko and Jasper Johns, or by British artists David Hockney and Peter Blake. Outside, the pedestrian Millennium Bridge (➤ 57) is London's first new span for a century.

WESTMINSTER ABBEY

It requires an effort to get there, but the very best time to be in the abbey is for the 8AM service in tiny St. Faith's Chapel, and then a wander in the silent nave and cloisters before the noisy tours arrive.

The kernel of London's second city It was Edward the Confessor who in the 11th century began the rebuilding of the modest Benedictine abbey church of St. Peter which was consecrated in 1065. The first sovereign to be crowned there was William the Conqueror, on Christmas Day 1066. Successive kings were patrons, as were the pilgrims who flocked to the Confessor's shrine. Henry III (1216–72) employed Master Henry de Reyns to re-begin the Gothic abbey that

The West Front

stands today, and Henry VII (1485–1509) built his Tudor chapel with its delicate fan vaulting. Since William I, all sovereigns have been crowned here—even after Henry VIII broke with Rome in 1533 and made himself head of the Church of England; and all were buried here up to George II (after which Windsor became the royal burial place ➤ 20–21).

Daunting riches The abbey is massive, full of monuments, and very popular. At the west door, enjoy the view and Master Henry's achievement, then look over the Victorian Gothic choir screen into Henry V's chantry. After seeing the chapels, the royal necropolis, and Poets' Corner, leave time for the peaceful cloisters.

HIGHLIGHTS

- Portrait of Richard II
- Mid-morning choral singing
- Sir Isaac Newton memorial
- Thornhill's window
- Henry VII's Chapel
- Edward the Confessor's Chapel
- St. Faith's Chapel
- Tile floor, Chapter House
- Little Cloister and College Garden
- Weekday sung evensong (except Wed) at 5PM

INFORMATION

- ✚ G7
- ✉ Broad Sanctuary, SW1
- ☎ 020 7222 5152
- ◉ Nave and Royal chapels Mon–Fri 9:30–3:45; Sat 9:30–1:45. Photography Wed 6PM–7PM. Chapter House, Pyx Chamber, Abbey Museum, and College Garden daily various hours. Closed before special services, Sun, Dec 24–28, Good Fri, and Commonwealth Observance Day.
- 🍴 Café in cloisters
- Ⓢ Westminster
- 🚆 Victoria
- ♿ Good
- 💲 Services free. Royal Chapels expensive
- ↔ Houses of Parliament (➤ 36)
- ❓ Guided tours

35

13

HOUSES OF PARLIAMENT

HIGHLIGHTS

- View from Westminster Bridge
- Statue of Oliver Cromwell
- Big Ben
- Richard I's equestrian statue
- Commons or Lords debates
- Line of Route Tours
- St. Stephen's Hall
- Westminster Hall
- State Opening of Parliament
- Jewel Tower

INFORMATION

✚ G7
✉ Westminster, SW1
☎ 020 7219 3000
  Commons 020 7219 4272
  Lords 020 7219 3107
  Jewel Tower 020 7222 2219
🕐 Parliament sits Mon, Tue, Thu 2:30; Wed, Fri 9:30. Closed hols and summer recesses (late Jul to mid-Oct).
  Jewel Tower Apr–Sep: daily 10–6. Oct–Mar: daily 10–4.
🚇 Westminster
🚉 Waterloo
♿ Parliament free. Line up (non-U.K. residents can apply for tickets from their embassy or consulate). Line of Route permits ✉ Public Information Office, House of Commons, 1 Derby Gate. Jewel Tower moderate
🔁 Westminster Abbey (➤ 35)
❓ State Opening of Parliament mid-Nov (➤ 22)

Big Ben is for many the symbol of London: they love its tower, its huge clear clockface, its thundering hour bell whose name is now given to the whole tower, and the way it glows like a reassuring beacon when illuminated at night.

Powerhouse for Crown and State   William the Conqueror made Westminster his seat of rule to watch over the London merchants (he also built the Tower of London ➤ 48). It was soon the center of government for England, then Britain, then a globe-encircling empire. It was also the principal home of the monarchs until Henry VIII moved to Whitehall.

Mother of parliaments   Here the foundations of Parliament were laid according to Edward I's Model Parliament of 1295; a combination of elected citizens, lords, and clergy. This developed into the House of Commons (elected Members of Parliament) and the House of Lords (unelected senior members of State and Church). Henry VIII's Reformation Parliament of 1529–36 ended Church domination of Parliament and made the Commons more powerful than the Lords.

A building fit for an empire   Having survived the Catholic conspiracy to blow up Parliament (on November 5, 1605, Guy Fawkes' night), almost all the buildings were destroyed by a fire in 1834. Kingdom and empire needed a new headquarters. With Charles Barry's plans and A. W. Pugin's detailed design, a masterpiece of Victorian Gothic was created. Behind the river facade decorated with statues of rulers, the Lords is on the left and the Commons on the right. If Parliament is in session, there is a flag on Victoria Tower or, at night, a light on Big Ben.

BANQUETING HOUSE

It is chilling to imagine Charles I calmly walking across the park from St. James's Palace to be beheaded outside the glorious hall built by his father. The magnificent ceiling was painted for Charles by Peter Paul Rubens.

London's most magnificent room This, all that remains of Whitehall Palace, was London's first building to be coated in smooth, white Portland stone. Designed by Inigo Jones and built between 1619 and 1622, it marked the beginning of James I's dream to replace the original sprawling Tudor palace with a 2,000-room Palladian masterpiece. In fact, it was only the banqueting hall that was built. Inside, the King hosted small parties in the crypt and presided over lavish court ceremonies upstairs.

The Rubens ceiling The stunning ceiling was commissioned by James's son, Charles I. Painted between 1634 and 1636 by Peter Paul Rubens, the leading baroque artist based in Antwerp, the panels celebrate James I, who was also James VI of Scotland. Nine allegorical paintings show the unification of Scotland and England and the joyous benefits of wise rule. Rubens was paid £3,000 and given a knighthood for the work.

The demise of Whitehall Palace This palace has brought a fair share of bad luck to its occupants. Cardinal Thomas Wolsey lived so ostentatiously that he fell from Henry VIII's favor. Henry moved in, making it his and his successors' main London royal residence. It was here that Charles I was beheaded on January 30, 1649, and William III suffered from the dank river air. A fire in 1698 wiped out the Tudor building, leaving only the stone Banqueting House.

HIGHLIGHTS

- Sculpted head of Charles I
- Weathercock put on the roof by James II
- Rubens ceiling
- Allegory of James I between Peace and Plenty
- Allegory of the birth and coronation of Charles I
- Nighttime concerts
- Whitehall river row house in Embankment Gardens
- The video and self-guiding audio tour

INFORMATION

- ⊞ G6
- ⊠ Whitehall, SW1
- ☎ 020 7930 4179
- ◷ Mon–Sat 10–5. Last admission 4:30. Closed Dec 24–Jan 1, public hols, and for government functions
- 🚇 Westminster, Charing Cross or Embankment
- ♿ None
- 🎫 Moderate
- ↔ St. James's Park (► 33), National Gallery (► 39), Cabinet War Rooms (► 50)
- ❓ Occasional concerts

Inigo Jones's facade

15

NATIONAL PORTRAIT GALLERY

HIGHLIGHTS

- *Self-portrait with Barbara Hepworth*, Ben Nicholson
- Icon-like *Richard II*
- Holbein's miniature of Thomas Cromwell
- *Samuel Pepys*, John Hayl
- *Queen Victoria*, Sir George Hayter
- *The Brontë Sisters*, Branwell Brontë
- *Isambard Kingdom Brunel*, John Callcott
- *Florence Nightingale*, William White
- *Sir Peter Hall*, Tom Phillips
- Using the self-guiding audio tour

INFORMATION

- 🔲 G5
- ✉ St. Martin's Place, WC2
- ☎ 020 7306 0055
- 🕐 Mon–Sat 10–6; Sun noon–6. Closed Dec 24–26, Jan 1, Good Fri, May Day
- 🚇 Leicester Square or Charing Cross
- 🚉 Charing Cross
- ♿ Good
- 🎫 Free except for special exhibitions
- ↔ National Gallery (▶ 39)
- ❓ Lectures, events

It is always fascinating to see what some- one famous looks like and how they chose to be painted—for instance, you would never expect Francis Drake to be in red courtier's, rather than sailor's, clothes.

A British record Founded in 1856 to collect portraits of the great and good in British life, and so inspire others to greatness, this now huge collection is the world's most comprehensive of its kind. There are oil paintings, watercolors, caricatures, silhouettes, and photographs.

Start at the top The galleries are arranged in chronological order, starting on the top floor (which can be reached by stairs or elevator). Henry VIII and some of his wives kick off a visual Who's Who of British history that moves through inventors, merchants, engineers, explorers, and empire builders to modern politicians, always accompanied by their observers, the writers. Isambard K. Brunel and Edward Jenner are here; so, too, are Robert Clive and Warren Hastings, of India, Winston Churchill, and Margaret Thatcher. There is Chaucer in his floppy hat, Kipling at his desk, and A. A. Milne with Christopher Robin and Winnie-the-Pooh on his knee. Some of the lesser-known sitters also merit a close look, such as the 18th-century group portrait of the remarkable and extensive Sharp Family, who formed an orchestra and played at Fulham every Sunday.

A modern record, too At first, the Victorians insisted upon entry only after death, but this rule has been broken. Among the many contemporary portraits, you may find those of the Princess Royal, Beatle Sir Paul McCartney, soccer player Bobby Charlton, Maggie Hambling's *Stephen Fry*, and Andy Warhol's *Joan Collins*.

NATIONAL GALLERY

The facades may be unexciting, but here is a collection of tip-top pictures—and for free, so you can drop in for a few minutes' peace in front of Leonardo da Vinci's cartoon in the Sainsbury Wing or Rubens's ravishing **Samson and Delilah.**

A quality collection Founded in 1824 with just 38 pictures, the National Gallery now has about 2,000 paintings, all on show. Spread throughout William Wilkins's neoclassical building and the new Sainsbury Wing extension (opened 1991), they provide an uncramped, extremely high-quality, concise panorama of European painting from Giotto to Cézanne. Most modern and British pictures are at the Tate Galleries (➤ 34).

Free from the start Unusually for a national painting collection, the nucleus is not royal but the collection of John Julius Angerstein, a self-made financier. From the start it was open to all, including children, free of charge (the British Museum charged at first), and provided a wide spectrum of British painting within a European context—aims that are still maintained. New arrivals include the Clarisse master, *Virgin and Child.*

A first visit To take advantage of the rich artistic panorama, why not choose a room from each of the four chronologically arranged sections? Early paintings by Duccio di Buoninsegna, Jan van Eyck, Piero della Francesca, and others fill the Sainsbury Wing. The West Wing has 16th-century pictures, including Michelangelo's *Entombment,* while the North Wing is devoted to 17th-century artists such as Van Dyck, Rubens, Rembrandt, Velàzquez, and painters of the Dutch school. Finally, the East Wing runs from Chardin through Gainsborough to Matisse and Picasso.

HIGHLIGHTS

- Cartoon, Leonardo da Vinci
- Pope Julius II, Raphael
- *The Arnolfini Wedding,* Van Eyck
- Equestrian portrait of Charles I by Van Dyck
- *The Triumph of Pan,* Poussin
- *Whistlejacket,* George Stubbs
- *The House of Cards,* Chardin
- *Mr and Mrs William Hallett,* Gainsborough
- *La Pointe de Hève,* Monet
- View from Wilkins's entrance

INFORMATION

- G6
- Trafalgar Square, WC2
- 020 7839 3321
- Mon, Tue, Thu–Sun 10–6; Wed 10–9. Closed Dec 24–26, Jan 1, Good Fri
- Brasserie, basement café
- Charing Cross or Leicester Square
- Charing Cross
- Excellent
- Free except for special exhibitions
- St. James's Park (➤ 33), National Portrait Gallery (➤ 38)
- Guided tours, lectures, films, picture identification service

39

COVENT GARDEN PIAZZA

HIGHLIGHTS

- Bedford arms and motto over the Market entrances
- St. Paul's Covent Garden
- 1920s and 1930s underground posters
- Craft stands in Apple Market
- The Royal Opera House
- Jubilee Hall Market
- How the underground works, London Transport Museum
- Charles H. Fox's make-up shop, Tavistock Street
- Neal Street, nearby

INFORMATION

➕ G5
✉ Covent Garden Piazza, WC2
🍴 Plentiful, all prices
Ⓒ Covent Garden
Ⓡ Charing Cross
♿ Good
🎫 Free except museums
↔ National Portrait Gallery
(➤ 38), Courtauld Gallery
(➤ 41), British Museum
(➤ 43), Dr. Johnson's
House (➤ 52)

London Transport Museum
✉ 39 Wellington Street, WC2
☎ 020 7379 6344
🕐 Mon–Thu, Sat, Sun 10–6;
Fri 11–6. Last admission
5:15. Closed Dec 24–26
🍴 Café
♿ Very good
🎫 Expensive
❓ Weekend guided tours, lectures, films, workshops

It is always fun to cut through the piazza, to see perhaps a family of clowns cavorting in front of St. Paul's Church, a busker cheering on the vendors, and people meeting up to enjoy the city.

London's first square Charles I was against expanding beyond the City but Francis Russell, the Earl of Bedford, owned a prime piece of land just west of it. Around 1630, the Earl paid the King £2,000 for a building license and used Inigo Jones to lay out London's first residential square. An instant success, it became a distinctive London feature.

Covent Garden When society left, the vegetable market moved in, together with taverns, gambling dens, and prostitutes. Charles Fowler's Central Market (1831) brought order, as did Floral, Flower, and Jubilee Halls, making this London's central fruit and vegetable

A Punch and Judy show

market until 1974. Locals saved the area from demolition, and today the restored halls and rebuilt Royal Opera House complex (➤ 54) make the piazza sparkle again.

London Transport Museum This tells the story of the world's largest urban public transportation system, which covers more than 500,000 miles. There are buttons to push and plenty of vehicles. Star attractions include the underground simulator, the touch screens in six languages, actors on the vehicles—and the shop.

COURTAULD GALLERY

These sumptuously decorated galleries hung with Impressionist paintings—Renoir's La Lôge, Manet's *Bar at the Folies-Bergère,* Cézannes, Gauguins, *and many more—are the perfect antidote to a gray, cloud-coated London day.*

One man's vision The industrialist Samuel Courtauld began collecting French Impressionist and Post-Impressionist paintings in 1921. Ten years later he founded the Courtauld Institute of Art. Using his own mansion designed by Robert Adam in Portman Square, he hoped that art history students would learn about paintings in the setting of fine architecture and furniture. In its new home on the Strand, the Courtauld fulfills his aim perfectly.

A palatial home A majestic, triple-arched gateway leads into Sir William Chambers's English Palladian government offices (1776–86). Ahead, the great courtyard is used for open-air theater and the riverside facade houses the Gilbert Collection of silver, gold, and mosaics. To the right, through a modest door, the Courtauld Collection fills a dozen lavishly decorated, restored rooms, once the home of the Royal Academy (▶ 51).

Six collections in one After Courtauld, five other collectors donated their art. Lord Lee of Fareham presented old masters and British works; art critic Roger Fry gave his collection; Sir Robert Witt gave his drawings (now the Witt Library, filling the vaults); the Mark Gambier-Parry Bequest includes Italian Renaissance panels, and Count Antoine Seilern's Prince Gate Collection includes baroque painters such as Rubens, Tiepolo, and Van Dyck. The small, beautiful rooms add an intimacy to your visit.

HIGHLIGHTS

- *Card Players*, Cézanne
- *Nevermore*, Gauguin
- *Peach Trees in Blossom*, van Gogh
- *Bar at the Folies-Bergère*, Manet
- *La Lôge*, Renoir
- Any of 32 Rubens paintings
- Beechey's portrait of Queen Charlotte
- Old master drawings
- Early Renaissance Gallery

INFORMATION

- G5
- Somerset House, Strand, WC2
- 020 7848 2526
- Mon–Sat 10–6; Sun 2–6. Last admission 5:15. Closed Dec 24–26
- Café
- Temple
- Blackfriars, Charing Cross
- Excellent
- Moderate
- Covent Garden Piazza (▶ 40), Sir John Soane's Museum (▶ 42), Dr. Johnson's House (▶ 52)
- Guided tours (pre-arranged), talks by students; summer concerts; prints and drawings study room

Top: detail, Gauguin's Nevermore

19

Sir John Soane's Museum

HIGHLIGHTS

- The Rake's Progress, The Election, Hogarth
- Sarcophagus of Seti I
- Lawrence's portrait of Soane
- Monk's Parlour
- Works by Turner, Canaletto
- Model Room

INFORMATION

- ⊞ G5
- ✉ 13 Lincoln's Inn Fields, WC2
- ☎ 020 7405 2107
- 🕐 Tue–Sat 10–5. 1st Tue of the month 6PM–9PM. Closed Dec 24–26, Jan 1, Good Fri
- 🚇 Holborn
- 🚊 Farringdon
- 🎟 Free
- ↔ Courtauld Gallery (➤ 41), British Museum (➤ 43), Dickens House (➤ 44)
- 🎧 Guided tours Sat 2:30

As you move about the gloriously over-furnished rooms of Soane's two houses—he outgrew one so built a second next door—and into the calm upstairs drawing room, his presence is so strong you feel you would not be surprised if he were there to greet you.

Soane the architect This double treasure-house in leafy Lincoln's Inn Fields, central London's largest square, is where the neoclassical architect Sir John Soane lived. First he designed No. 12 and lived there from 1792. Then he bought No. 13 next door, rebuilt it with cunningly propor-tioned rooms, and lived there from 1813 until his death in 1837. Meanwhile, he also designed Holy Trinity on Marylebone Road (1824–8), and parts of the Treasury, Whitehall. His model for his masterpiece, the (destroyed) Bank of England, is here (re-created rooms now form the bank's museum ➤ 50). No. 14 opens as a center for Adam Studies in 2004.

Soane the collector Soane was an avid collec-tor. He found that every art object could inspire his work, so his rooms were a visual reference library. Hogarth's paintings unfold from the walls in layers. There are so many sculptures, paint-ings, and antiquities that unless you keep your eyes peeled you will miss a Watteau drawing, a Greek vase, or something better.

The ghost of Soane Sir John's ingenious designs pervade every room, as do the stories of his passion for collecting. For example, when an Egyptian sarc-ophagus arrived, he gave a three-day party in its honor.

Behind the facade a labyrinth of rooms houses a bizarre collection

BRITISH MUSEUM

It's fun to choose your own seven wonders of the world in the British Museum. The bronzes from the Indian Chola dynasty and the lion-filled reliefs that once lined an Assyrian palace may well be on everyone's list, but the others will vary.

The physician founder   Sir Hans Sloane, after whom Sloane Square is named, was a fashionable London physician, "interested in the whole of human knowledge" and an avid collector of everything from plants to prints. When he died in 1753 aged 92 he left his collection of more than 80,000 objects to the nation on condition that it was given a permanent home. Thus began the British Museum, opened in 1759 in a 17th-century mansion, Britain's first public museum and now its largest, covering 13½ acres.

It grew and it grew   To Sloane's collection were added many others. Kings George II, III, and IV made magnificent gifts, as did other monarchs. These, with the Townley and Elgin Marbles, burst the building's seams and the architect Robert Smirke designed a grand new museum, completed by his son, Sydney, in 1857. Even so, because the booty from expeditions and excavations poured in continuously, the Natural History collections went to South Kensington (➤ 26). With the departure of the British Library (➤ 54) to St. Pancras in 1998, the central Great Court has been redeveloped and the Sainsbury Galleries built for the African collections.

Coming to grips with the British Museum   A good way to explore "that old curiosity shop in Great Russell Street" is to pick up a plan in the Great Court, see what special events are on, choose at the most three rooms to see, and set off to find them. For peace and quiet, go early.

HIGHLIGHTS

- Oriental antiquities
- Sainsbury Galleries
- Rosetta Stone
- Current prints and drawings
- Islamic Art
- Mildenhall and Sutton Hoo treasures
- Elgin Marbles
- Assyrian and Egyptian rooms
- Roman Britain Gallery
- Norman Foster's Great Court redevelopment

INFORMATION

- ✚ G4
- ✉ Great Russell Street, WC1 (another entrance in Montague Place)
- ☎ 020 7636 1555
- 🕐 Mon–Sat 10–5; Sun 2:30–6. 1st Tue of the month 6PM–9PM. Closed Dec 24–26, Jan 1, Good Fri, May Day
- 🍽 Restaurant, café
- Ⓤ Holborn or Tottenham Court Road
- ♿ Very good
- 💷 Free except for some temporary exhibitions, tours, and late openings
- ↔ Covent Garden Piazza (➤ 40), Percival David Foundation of Chinese Art (➤ 51)
- ❓ Guided tours, talks, lectures

21

DICKENS HOUSE

HIGHLIGHTS

- Dickens's study
- Drawing Room
- Original manuscript of *Oliver Twist*
- Copy of *David Copperfield* found with the possessions of Scott of the Antarctic
- Original manuscript of *Pickwick Papers*
- Dickens's court suit
- "Phiz" illustrations
- Guided Dickens walks

INFORMATION

- H4
- 48 Doughty Street, WC1
- 020 7405 2127
- Mon–Sat 10–5. Closed Dec 25–Jan 4 and some public hols
- Russell Square, Chancery Lane, or King's Cross
- King's Cross
- Few
- Moderate
- Sir John Soane's Museum (➤ 42), British Museum (➤ 43), Percival David Foundation of Chinese Art (➤ 51)
- Information on regular Dickens walks

Standing beside Dickens's desk and chair in the house where he and his young wife lived, it is easy to imagine him going off on his long London walks to research deprived Victorian life while he was writing Oliver Twist.

Dickens's London homes Of Charles Dickens's many London homes, this is the only survivor. He lived here between 1837 and 1839, moving from Furnival's Inn, Holborn, after he married, and leaving when his growing family forced him to go to a larger house in Devonshire Terrace. The Doughty Street house is part of a typical flat-fronted, Regency row house, set in a wide and handsome Georgian avenue that, like the nearby Bloomsbury Square, would have had gates at either end manned by liveried porters, and mewslanes for servants and deliveries.

Dickens at Doughty Street Here Dickens completed *Pickwick Papers*, wrote *Oliver Twist* and *Nicholas Nickleby*, and began *Barnaby Rudge*. Here, too, Dickens emerged from his pseudonym of "Boz" into the literary limelight—there are some marked-up prompt copies for his legendary literary readings. Other Dickens memorabilia includes a Fagin toby jug.

The Dickens Fellowship This society, which bought the house in 1924 and restored the drawing room to its original decor, cares for the world's most comprehensive Dickens library and many Dickens-related portraits, letters, and manuscripts. Do not miss Harlot Knight Brown's "Phiz" illustrations, and a newly acquired writing desk and three portraits. If you want to get under Dickens's skin, visit the house and then join a guided walk (➤ 19) to explore a bit of his London.

ST. PAUL'S CATHEDRAL

To sneak into St. Paul's for afternoon evensong, and sit gazing up at the mosaics as the choir's voices soar, is to savor a moment of absolute peace and beauty.

Wren's London After the restoration of the monarchy in 1660, artistic patronage bloomed under Charles II. Then, when the Great Fire of London destroyed four-fifths of the City in 1666, Christopher Wren took center stage, being appointed King's Surveyor-General in 1669, aged just 37. The spires, towers, and steeples of his 51 new churches (23 still stand) surrounded his masterpiece, St. Paul's.

The fifth St. Paul's This cathedral church for the diocese of London was founded in AD 604 by King Ethelbert of Kent. The first four churches burned down. Wren's, built in stone and paid for with a special coal tax, was the first English cathedral built by a single architect, the only one with a dome, and the only one in the English baroque style. The funerals of Admiral Lord Nelson, the Duke of Wellington, and Sir Winston Churchill were held here; statues and memorials of Britain's famous crowd the interior and crypt.

The great climb The 530 steps to the top are worth the effort. Shallow steps rise to

the Whispering Gallery for good views of Thornhill's dome frescoes and Richmond and Salviati's Victorian mosaics. The external Stone Gallery has telescopes and benches; above is the Golden Gallery. Go early or late to avoid crowds.

HIGHLIGHTS

- Sung evensong
- Frescoes and mosaics
- Wren's Great Model in the triforium (upstairs)
- Triple-layered dome weighing 76,000 tons
- Jean Tijou's sanctuary gates
- Wellington's memorial
- *Light of the World*, Holman Hunt
- The great climb
- Wren's epitaph under the dome

INFORMATION

- ➕ J5
- ✉ St. Paul's Churchyard, EC4
- ☎ 020 7236 4128
- 🕐 Mon–Sat 8:30–4. Galleries Mon–Sat 10–5. Services Mon–Sat 5; Sun 11, 3:15
- 🍴 Refectory in the crypt
- Ⓜ St. Paul's or Mansion House
- 🚇 City Thameslink or Cannon Street
- ♿ Very good
- 💷 Moderate. Galleries extra
- ↔ Museum of London (► 47), Bank of England Museum (► 50), Dr. Johnson's House (► 52), St. Margaret, Lothbury (► 55), Tate Gallery of Modern Art (► 54)
- ❓ Guided tours Mon–Sat 11, 11:30, 1:30, 2; bell-ringing practice some Tue; organ recitals; masses in Jul

45

23

St. Bartholomew-the-Great

INFORMATION

- ✠ J4
- ✉ West Smithfield, EC1
- ☎ 020 7606 5171
- 🕐 Mon–Fri 8:30–5 (winter: 8:30–4); Sat 10:30–1:30; Sun 2–6.
  Sun services 9AM, 11AM (choral), 6:30PM (choral)
- Ⓔ Barbican, Farringdon, or St. Paul's
- 🚇 Farringdon
- ♿ Good
- 💷 Free (donation encouraged)
- ↔ St. Paul's Cathedral (➤ 45), Museum of London (➤ 47)
- ❓ Exceptional choir

A Sunday evening spent at St. Bartholomew's is truly memorable: While trucks arrive at Smithfield's meat market, you can answer the ringing bells and pass under the great stone arch into a hidden, medieval world for beautifully sung evensong.

A court jester for founder Henry I's court jester, Rahere, became an Augustinian canon. While on pilgrimage to Rome he was cured of malaria, had a vision of St. Bartholomew, and took a vow. On his return, the King gave him land to found St. Bartholomew's Hospital and Priory—London's first hospital but one of four monasteries in the area.

London's oldest church Rahere's priory church, built in 1123, is London's oldest surviving church, the City's only 12th-century monastic church, and its best surviving piece of large-scale Romanesque architecture. The remains (the nave and cloisters are gone) give an idea of the magnificence of London's dozen or so medieval monastic churches.

Entering a different world The church lies through a 13th-century stone arch topped by a Tudor gatehouse, which once led into the great priory church's west end. Today, a path runs the length of what was the ten-bay nave down to the present west door. Here is the choir, the ambulatory, and the Lady Chapel (built by Rahere), whose roofs are supported by honey-colored walls and sturdy, circular columns. The minimal decoration makes the impact all the more powerful. Two tombs sit uneasily together here: those of the founder, Rahere (*d*1143; tomb 1404), and of the destroyer, Richard Rich, who bought the building from Henry VIII after the dissolution of the monasteries.

MUSEUM OF LONDON

A visit here is easily the best way to cruise through London's 2,000 years of history, pausing to see a Roman shoe, the Lord Mayor's State Coach, or an old shop counter; and it is even built on top of the West Gate of London's Roman fort.

A museum for London This is the world's largest and most comprehensive city museum, opened in 1975 in a building by Powell and Moya. The collection combines the old Guildhall Museum's City antiquities with the London Museum's costumes and other culturally related objects. Plenty of building work and redevelopment in the City of London in the 1980s, allied with increased awareness about conservation, has ensured a steady flow of archeological finds into the collection.

A museum about London The story of London is long and can be confusing. The building is, appropriately, in the barbican of the Roman fort, and the rooms are laid out chronologically to keep the story clear. Starting with prehistoric and Roman times (do not miss the peep-hole window down to 2nd-century barbican remains), the rooms work through the medieval, Tudor, and Stuart period. A highlight here is the re-enactment of the Great Fire of London in 1666. The Georgian, Victorian, and 20th-century rooms mix low life with high, ranging from Newgate Gaol and the Blitz Experience to Spitalfields silks, and high-fashion stores, and ending with the London Now Gallery.

A museum about Londoners People make a city, so in every room it is Londoners who are really telling the story, whether it is through their Roman storage jars, their Tudor leather clothes, or their Suffragette posters.

HIGHLIGHTS

- Neolithic bowl
- Roman letter addressed "Londinio"
- Roman wall remnants
- Viking grave
- Fragments from the Eleanor Cross
- Tudor jewelry
- Model of Tudor London
- Pepys's chess set
- 15th-century paneled room
- London Now Gallery

INFORMATION

- ✚ J4
- ✉ 150 London Wall, EC2
- ☎ 020 7600 3699
- 🕐 Tue–Sat 10–5:50; Sun noon–5:50. Closed Dec 24–26, Jan 1
- 🍴 Restaurant, café
- Ⓢ Barbican, Moorgate, or St. Paul's
- 🚆 Moorgate, Farringdon, Liverpool Street, or City Thameslink
- ♿ Excellent
- 💷 Moderate. All tickets valid for one year
- ↔ St. Paul's Cathedral (► 45), St. Bartholomew-the-Great (► 46), Barbican (► 78–79)
- ❓ Lectures, gallery talks, performances, seminars, workshops; "Made in London" film series

Mural depicting a scene from the Great Fire

25

H.M. THE TOWER OF LONDON

HIGHLIGHTS

- Medieval Palace
- Raleigh's room
- Imperial State Crown
- Tower ravens
- Grand Punch Bowl, 1829
- St. John's Chapel

INFORMATION

- ✚ K5
- ☎ 020 7709 0765
- 🕐 Apr–Oct: daily 10–6:30.
  Nov–Mar: daily 9:30–6:30.
  Closed Dec 24–26, Jan 1
- 🍴 Cafés
- 🚇 Tower Hill
- 🚉 Fenchurch Street, Cannon
  Street, or London Bridge
- ♿ Excellent for Jewel House
- 💷 Very expensive
- ↔ Design Museum (➤ 50),
  H.M.S. *Belfast* (➤ 58),
  Tower Bridge Museum
  (➤ 57)
- ❓ Tours every 30 minutes

A "Beefeater"

The medieval palace, where Edward I lived at the end of the 13th century, brings the Tower alive as the royal palace and place of pageantry it was; for some, it's more interesting than the Crown Jewels.

Medieval fortress The Tower of London is Britain's best medieval fortress. William the Conqueror (1066–87) began it as a show of brute force, and Edward I (1272–1307) completed it. William's Caen stone White Tower, built within old Roman walls, was an excellent defense: it was 90 feet high, with walls 15 feet thick, and space for soldiers, servants, and nobles. Henry III began the Inner Wall, the moat, his own water-gate—and the royal zoo. Edward I completed the Inner Wall, built the Outer Wall, several towers, and Traitor's Gate, and moved the mint and Crown Jewels here from Westminster.

Scenes of splendor and horror Stephen (1135–54) was the first king to live here, James I (1603–25) the last. From here Edward I went into procession to his coronation and Henry VIII paraded through the city bedecked in cloth of gold. Here the Barons seized the Tower to force King John to put his seal to the Magna Carta in 1215; and here two princes were murdered while their uncle was being crowned Richard III. Since 1485 it has been guarded by Yeoman Warders or "Beefeaters".

Seven centuries of history The Tower has been palace, fortress, state prison, and execution site. There is much to see. Come early and see the Crown Jewels and the Crowns and Diamonds Exhibition, then take a break along the Wharf.

LONDON's *best*

MUSEUMS & GALLERIES

Dulwich Picture Gallery

Dulwich Picture Gallery's magnificent core collection of 400 paintings was assembled for the King of Poland's projected national gallery. When the king abdicated, the collection was offered unsuccessfully to Britain for the same purpose. The art dealer who put it together, Noel Desenfans, gave it to Sir Francis Bourgeois, who donated it to Dulwich College. Housed in a building designed by Sir John Soane, and opened in 1814, it was England's first public art gallery.

The Edwardian Room, in the Geffrye Museum

BANK OF ENGLAND MUSEUM
See how Britain's monetary system and banking ideas have grown since 1694.
➕ J5 ✉ Bartholomew Lane, EC3 ☎ 020 7601 5545 ⏰ Mon–Fri 10–5 🚇 Bank 💷 Free

CABINET WAR ROOMS
The underground headquarters for Sir Winston Churchill's War Cabinet during World War II.
➕ G6 ✉ Clive Steps, King Charles Street, SW1 ☎ 020 7930 6961 ⏰ Oct–Mar: daily 10–6. Apr–Sep: daily 9:30–6 🚇 St. James's Park or Westminster 💷 Expensive

DESIGN MUSEUM
Founded by design guru Sir Terence Conran (➤ 9) to stimulate design awareness. Good shop.
➕ L6 ✉ Butler's Wharf, Shad Thames, SE1 ☎ 020 7403 6933 ⏰ Daily 11:30–6 🍴 Café, restaurant 🚇 Tower Hill or London Bridge 🚉 London Bridge 💷 Expensive

DULWICH PICTURE GALLERY
European art. See panel.
➕ Off map at K10 ✉ College Road, SE21 ☎ 020 8693 5254 ⏰ Tue–Fri 10–5; Sat 11–5; Sun 2–5 🍴 Summer tea tent 🚉 North or West Dulwich 💷 Moderate. Free on Fri

GEFFRYE MUSEUM
Almshouses furnished in period style, 1550–1950.
➕ K3 ✉ Kingsland Road, E2 ☎ 020 7739 9893 ⏰ Tue–Sat 10–5; Sun, public hols 2–5PM. Closed Good Fri 🍴 Café 🚇 Old Street, bus 22A, 243; Liverpool Street, bus 22B, 149 💷 Free

HAYWARD GALLERY
Major venue to art exhibitions.
➕ H6 ✉ South Bank, SE1 ☎ 020 7928 3144 🕐 Daily 10–6.
During exhibitions Tue, Wed 10–8 🍴 Café 🚇 Waterloo
🚉 Waterloo 💷 Moderate

HOUSE MUSEUMS (▶ 52)

IMPERIAL WAR MUSEUM
Focuses on the social impact of 20th-century war-
fare through film, painting, and sound archives.
➕ H7 ✉ Lambeth Road, SE1 ☎ 020 7416 5000 🕐 Daily
10–6 🍴 Restaurant, café 🚇 Lambeth North, Elephant & Castle
or Waterloo 🚉 Waterloo 💷 Expensive

LONDON AQUARIUM
An aquatic spectacular. Follow the story of a
stream, an ocean, a coral reef, and more.
➕ G6 ✉ County Hall, Riverside Building, Westminster Bridge
Road, SE1 ☎ 020 7967 8000 🕐 Mon–Fri 10–6; Sat, Sun
9:30–6. Last admission 1 hour before closing 🍴 Café
🚇 Westminster 💷 Expensive

**PERCIVAL DAVID
FOUNDATION OF CHINESE ART**
Sublime Chinese ceramics.
➕ G4 ✉ 53 Gordon Square, WC1 ☎ 020 7387 3909
🕐 Mon–Fri 10:30–5 🚇 Russell Square 💷 Free

PHOTOGRAPHERS' GALLERY
Contemporary photos in the heart of London.
➕ G5 ✉ 5–8 Great Newport Street, WC2 ☎ 020 7831 1772
🕐 Mon–Sat 11–6; Sun 12–6 🚇 Leicester Square 💷 Free

POLLOCK TOY MUSEUM
Two houses full of dolls, teddy bears, puppets, and
Mr Pollock's workshop, where he made his toy
theaters—still sold at the shop.
➕ F4 ✉ 1 Scala Street, W1 ☎ 020 7636 3452 🕐 Mon–Sat
10–5 🚇 Goodge Street 💷 Inexpensive

ROYAL ACADEMY
Major art shows, plus the annual Summer Exhibition.
Don't miss rooftop Sackler Galleries.
➕ F6 ✉ Burlington House, Piccadilly, W1 ☎ 020 7300 8000
🕐 Daily 10–6. Some late openings. Closed Good Fri 🍴 Restaurant,
café 🚇 Green Park or Piccadilly 💷 Expensive

TOWER BRIDGE MUSEUM (▶ 57)

WALLACE COLLECTION
Artworks in an 18th-century town house. See panel.
➕ E5 ✉ Hertford House, Manchester Square, W1 ☎ 020
7935 0687 🕐 Mon–Sat 10–5; Sun 2–5 🚇 Bond Street 💷 Free

WHITECHAPEL ART GALLERY
The hub of vibrant East End art activities.
➕ L5 ✉ 80 Whitechapel High Street, E1 ☎ 020 7522 7888
🕐 Tue, Thu–Sun 11–5; Wed 11–8 🍴 Café 🚇 Aldgate East 💷 Free

*The Pacific Tank at the
London Aquarium*

The Wallace Collection

The Wallace Collection is the
product of five generations of
discerning art collectors. The
1st Marquess of Hertford bought
Ramsays and Canalettos; the
2nd acquired Gainsborough's *Mrs
Robinson*; the 3rd preferred
Sèvres and Dutch 17th-century
pictures; and the 4th, in Paris
during the Revolution, snapped
up quality French art. His
illegitimate son, Sir Richard
Wallace, added his own Italian
majolica, Renaissance armor,
bronzes, and gold.

51

HOUSE MUSEUMS

Dr. Johnson's House

Leighton House

Lord Leighton made his reputation when Queen Victoria bought one of his paintings. George Aitchison then designed his home-cum-studio (1861–6). The fashionable painter and esthete gave the rooms rich red walls edged with ebonized wood. Their centerpiece is the Arab Hall, one of London's most exotic rooms, lined with Persian and Saracenic blue and green tiles collected by Leighton during his travels.

APSLEY HOUSE (WELLINGTON MUSEUM)
Splendid mansion built for Arthur Wellesley, the Duke of Wellington (1759–1852).
➕ E6 ✉ Hyde Park Corner, SW1 ☎ 020 7499 5676
🕐 Tue–Sun 11–5 🚇 Hyde Park Corner 💷 Expensive

CARLYLE'S HOUSE
Thomas Carlyle, Scottish philosopher and historian, lived here from 1834 until his death in 1881.
➕ D8 ✉ 24 Cheyne Row, SW3 ☎ 020 7352 7087 🕐 Apr–Oct: Wed–Sun, public hols 11–5. Last admission 4:30. Closed Nov–Mar
🚇 Sloane Square 💷 Moderate

CHISWICK HOUSE
Lord Burlington's exquisite country villa (1725–9), whose formal garden is an integral part of his design. Don't miss a stroll along nearby Chiswick Mall.
➕ Off map at A8 ✉ Burlington Lane, W4 ☎ 020 8995 0508
🕐 Apr–Oct: daily 10–6. Nov–Mar: Wed–Sun 10–4 🍴 Café
🚇 Turnham Green 🚂 Chiswick 💷 Moderate

DR. JOHNSON'S HOUSE
Dr. Samuel Johnson lived here between 1749 and 1759 while compiling his dictionary.
➕ H5 ✉ 17 Gough Square EC4 ☎ 020 7353 3745 🕐 May–Sep: Mon–Sat 11–5:30. Oct–Apr: Mon–Sat 11–5 🚇 Chancery Lane or Blackfriars 🚂 Blackfriars 💷 Moderate

HAM HOUSE
Thameside mansion dating from 1610 refurbished in baroque style. Meticulously re-created 17th-century garden.
➕ Off map at A10 ✉ Ham, Richmond, Surrey ☎ 020 8940 1950
🕐 House Apr–Oct: Sat–Wed 1–5. Closed Nov–Mar. Gardens Sat–Wed 10:30–6 (or dusk) 🍴 Restaurant 🚇 Richmond, then bus 371
💷 Expensive

LEIGHTON HOUSE
See panel.
➕ B7 ✉ 12 Holland Park Road, W14 ☎ 020 7602 3316
🕐 Mon–Sat 10–5:30 🚇 High Street Kensington 💷 Free

SUTTON HOUSE (► 60)

WALLACE COLLECTION (► 51)

STATUES & MONUMENTS

BURGHERS OF CALAIS
Auguste Rodin's muscular bronze citizens (1915).
⊞ G7 ✉ Victoria Tower Gardens, SW1 🚇 Westminster

CHARLES I
This superb equestrian statue of Charles I was made
by Hubert Le Sueur in 1633.
⊞ G6 ✉ South side of Trafalgar Square 🚇 Charing Cross
🚊 Charing Cross

DUKE OF WELLINGTON
The only London hero to have three equestrian
statues: the others are in St. Paul's Cathedral and
outside the Duke's home, Apsley House (➤ 52).
⊞ J5 ✉ Opposite the Bank of England, EC2 🚇 Bank

EROS
Alfred Gilbert's memorial (1893) to the philanthropic
7th Earl of Shaftesbury (1801–85) actually portrays
the Angel of Christian Charity, not Eros.
⊞ F5 ✉ Piccadilly Circus, W1 🚇 Piccadilly Circus

MONUMENT
Wren's 202-foot Doric column commemorates the
Great Fire (1666). Worth climbing the dark
corkscrew of 311 steps for the view.
⊞ K5 ✉ Monument Street, EC3 🚇 Monument

NELSON'S COLUMN
Horatio, Viscount Nelson (1758–1805) went up on to
his 172-foot column in 1843; the hero died as he
defeated the French and Spanish at Trafalgar.
⊞ G6 ✉ Trafalgar Square 🚇 Charing Cross 🚊 Charing Cross

OLIVER CROMWELL
King-like Cromwell, Lord Protector of England from
1653 to 1658, looks across Parliament Square.
⊞ G7 ✉ Houses of Parliament 🚇 Westminster

PETER PAN
George Frampton's statue (1912) of J. M. Barrie's
creation, the boy who never grew up.
⊞ C6 ✉ Long Water, Kensington Gardens 🚇 Lancaster Gate

QUEEN ALEXANDRA
This art nouveau bronze designed by Alfred Gilbert,
a memorial to Edward VII's Danish-born wife, was
commissioned by her daughter-in-law, Queen Mary.
⊞ F6 ✉ Marlborough Road, SW1 🚇 Green Park

SIR ARTHUR SULLIVAN
William Goscombe John's bronze of the operetta
composer Sir Arthur Sullivan (1842–1900).
⊞ G5 ✉ Embankment Gardens 🚇 Embankment

Broadgate Centre

Part of the rampant
redevelopment of the City in the
1980s, Broadgate (➤ 54) was
exceptional for its commissioning
of public art. *Fulcrum* by Richard
Serra—vast steel sheets
tentatively resting against each
other—mark the Broadgate
square entrance. Beyond are
Barry Flanagan's *Leaping Hare on
Crescent and Bell* and George
Segal's *Rush Hour*. In the center
of Broadgate is the circular
Arena, which becomes an outdoor
ice rink in winter. Around its edge
are chic restaurants, wine bars,
and some shops.

*Peter Pan in Kensington
Gardens*

MODERN BUILDINGS

Designer store interiors

Sophisticated consumers have inspired retailers to create a stylish ambience in which to shop. Eva Jiricna has remodeled the Joseph shops (✉ 16 and 26 Sloane Street, SW1 and others) with her signature staircase, cable balustrades, and polished white plaster walls. Stanton Williams revamped Issey Miyake (✉ 270 Brompton Road, SW3), Branson Coates did Katharine Hamnett (✉ 20 Sloane Square, SW1) and Jigsaw (✉ 9 Argyll Street, W1 and others), and Wickham & Associates made Fifth Floor Harvey Nichols (► 71) a foodie's wonderland.

Broadgate

BROADGATE
This 29-acre mall and office development (1984–91) is distinguished by its impressive facades, street sculptures, open-air ice rink (Oct–Apr), and lunchtime events (summer). The architects were Arup Associates, Skidmore, Owings & Merrill, Inc. (► 53 panel).
✚ K4 ✉ EC2 ☎ 020 7505 4000 ⏱ 24 hours 🍴 Many 🚇 Liverpool Street

BRITISH LIBRARY
Colin St. John Wilson's redbrick home for the nation's books, with public galleries and piazza.
✚ G3 ✉ 96 Euston Road, NW1 ☎ 020 7412 7000 ⏱ Mon, Wed, Thu 9:30–6; Tue 9:30–8; Fri, Sat 9:30–5; Sun 11–5 🍴 Café, restaurant 🚇 Kings Cross 🎫 Free ↔ Millennium Bridge and Millennium Dome (► 57)

CANARY WHARF
César Pelli's soaring, blue-topped tower—the first to be clad in stainless steel—dominates Canary Wharf; Pelli describes it as "a square prism with pyramidal top in the traditional form of the obelisk." Buildings by other international architects surround it.
✚ Off map at N6 ✉ 1 Canada Square, Canary Wharf, Isle of Dogs, E14 ⏱ Public spaces are open, not buildings 🚇 Canary Wharf

ROYAL OPERA HOUSE
Dixon Jones and BDP have created three theaters and a huge lobby on a large site, incorporating the old opera house and Floral Hall.
✚ G5 ✉ Bow Street, WC2 ☎ 020 7240 1200 ⏱ All day 🍴 Café 🎫 Free during day, entry by ticket at night 🚇 Covent Garden

SACKLER GALLERIES
At Foster Associates' dazzling, airy rooftop galleries, light-sensitive louvers automatically control sunlight through fretted-glass windows.
✚ F6 ✉ Royal Academy (► 51)

TATE GALLERY OF MODERN ART (► 34)
Gilbert Scott's riverside power station transformed by Herzog and de Meuron into the perfect setting for contemporary art.
✚ J6 ✉ Bankside, SE1 🚇 Southwark, Blackfriars, London Bridge

WATERLOO INTERNATIONAL STATION
Designed by Nicholas Grimshaw and Partners and built to handle up to 15 million passengers a year, this is one of the world's longest railroad stations. The viaduct structure for five new tracks is spanned by a dramatic, glazed bowstring arch.
✚ H6 ✉ SE1 ⏱ Public space 🍴 Many 🚇 Waterloo

CHURCHES & CATHEDRALS

See Top 25 Sights for
COVENT GARDEN (▶ 40)
H.M. TOWER OF LONDON (▶ 48)
ST. BARTHOLOMEW-THE-GREAT (▶ 46)
ST. PAUL'S CATHEDRAL (▶ 45)
WESTMINSTER ABBEY (▶ 35)

ALL-HALLOWS-BY-THE-TOWER
Begun about 1000, the church contains a Roman pavement and a carving by Grinling Gibbons.
➕ K5 ✉ Byward Street, EC3 ☎ 020 7481 2928 🕐 Church Mon–Sat 9–6; Sun 10–5. Undercroft Museum daily 10–4:30 🚇 Tower Hill 🎧 Charge for self-guiding audio tour

CHELSEA OLD CHURCH
Begun in 1157 but much rebuilt. One of the best series of monuments in a London parish church.
➕ D8 ✉ Old Church Street, SW3 ☎ 020 7352 5627 🕐 Daily 9:30–1, 2–4:30 🚇 Sloane Square 🎫 Free

ORATORY OF ST. PHILIP NERI
Also known as the Brompton or London Oratory. Fine baroque interior.
➕ D7 ✉ Brompton Road, SW7 ☎ 020 7589 4811 🕐 Daily 6:30AM–8PM 🚇 South Kensington 🎫 Free

ST. ETHELDREDA'S CHAPEL
This Gothic chapel survives from the Bishops of Ely's medieval town house.
➕ H4 ✉ Ely Place, EC1 ☎ 020 7405 1061 🕐 Daily 7:30–7 🚇 Chancery Lane or Farringdon 🚊 Farringdon 🎫 Donation encouraged

ST. JAMES'S, PICCADILLY
Wren's chic church (1682–4) for local aristocracy has a sumptuous interior.
➕ F6 ✉ Piccadilly, SW1 ☎ 020 7734 4511 🕐 Apr–Sep: daily 8:30–7. Oct–Mar: daily 9–6 🍴 Café 🚇 Piccadilly Circus 🎫 Donation encouraged

ST. MARGARET, LOTHBURY
Wren's church (1686–90) retains its huge carved screen with soaring eagle and carved pulpit tester.
➕ J5 ✉ Lothbury, EC2 ☎ 020 7606 8330 🕐 Mon–Fri 8–5 🚇 Bank 🎫 Donation encouraged

TEMPLE CHURCH
Begun about 1160, this private chapel has a circular plan inspired by Jerusalem's Dome of the Rock. Effigies honor the Knights Templar, protectors of pilgrims to the Holy Land.
➕ H5 ✉ Inner Temple, EC4 ☎ 020 7353 1736 🕐 Wed–Sat 10–4; Sun services for worship. Closed for private functions 🚇 Temple 🎫 Free

Chapels Royal
London's five Chapels Royal are at St. James's Palace, Queen's Chapel, the Tower (St. Peter ad Vincula and St. John's), and Hampton Court Palace. The best services to attend are at St. Peter ad Vincula, St. James's Palace, and Hampton Court, as each retains a lavish, courtly atmosphere and has a superb choir.

The Oratory of St. Philip Neri (Brompton Oratory), by Herbert Gribble (1876)

GREEN SPACES

London is almost 11 percent parkland and has 67 square miles of green space, including the nine royal parks, former royal hunting grounds.

See Top 25 Sights for
HAMPSTEAD HEATH (➤ 29)
KENSINGTON GARDENS (➤ 25)
REGENT'S PARK (➤ 30)
ROYAL BOTANICAL GARDENS, KEW (➤ 24)
ST. JAMES'S PARK (➤ 33)

BUNHILL FIELDS
Leafy City oasis, where trees shade the tombs of Blake and Defoe.
➕ J4 ✉ City Road, EC1 🕐 Daily 7:30–dusk 🚇 Old Street
✋ Free

Riders in Rotten Row, Hyde Park

GREEN PARK
Peaceful royal park.
➕ F6 ✉ SW1 ☎ 020 7930 1793 🕐 Daily dawn–dusk 🚇 Green Park or Hyde Park Corner
✋ Free

GREENWICH (➤ 20)

HOLLAND PARK
Woodland and open lawns fill 54 acres around Holland House.
➕ A6 ✉ W11 ☎ 020 7471 9813 🕐 Daily 8–dusk 🍴 Restaurant, café 🚇 Holland Park
✋ Free

Royal parks

The nine royal parks, mostly former hunting grounds, are Londoners' substitute backyards. They also act as the city's green lungs. Many are also important bird sanctuaries. Their open spaces, woods, meadows, ponds, and wide variety of mature trees have been the setting for events ranging from the Great Exhibition of 1851 to riotous demonstrations. Today, they are places to meet, picnic, play games and, in summer, enjoy a concert or a play.

HOLY TRINITY, BROMPTON
A large, tree-shaded, airy churchyard, useful between South Kensington Museum visits.
➕ D7 ✉ Brompton Road, SW7 🕐 24 hours 🚇 South Kensington
✋ Free

HYDE PARK
One of London's largest open spaces, tamed by 18th-century royalty.
➕ D6 ✉ W2 ☎ 020 7298 2000 🕐 Daily 5–midnight
🍴 Restaurant, café 🚇 Marble Arch, Lancaster Gate, Knightsbridge, or Hyde Park Corner ✋ Free

PRIMROSE HILL
One of London's best panoramas.
➕ D2 ✉ NW3 ☎ 020 7486 7905 🕐 Daily dawn–midnight
🚇 St. John's Wood or Camden Town ✋ Free

RUSSELL SQUARE
Lawns, trees, and café near the British Museum.
➕ G4 ✉ WC1 🕐 Daily 7–dusk 🍴 Café 🚇 Russell Square
✋ Free

THAMES SIGHTS

London grew up around the Thames. As the port expanded, so did London's wealth and power. The Thames was its main thoroughfare, used by all.

BAZALGETTE'S EMBANKMENT (➤ 12)

CLEOPATRA'S NEEDLE
The 86-foot pink-granite obelisk made in 1450 BC records the triumphs of Rameses the Great.
➕ G6 ✉ Victoria Embankment, WC2 🚇 Embankment or Charing Cross 🎫 Free

DOCKLANDS
Waterparks, the high-level Docklands Light Railway, Island Gardens, Museum in Docklands, and more.
✉ Stretches eastward from Tower of London to Royal Docks ⏱ 24 hours for public areas 🚇 Use DLR to explore 🎫 Free

DRAGONS ON THE EMBANKMENT
The silver cast-iron dragons (1849) mark the City of London boundary.
➕ H5 ✉ Victoria Embankment, WC2 🚇 Temple

MILLENNIUM DOME
Richard Rogers and Partners' huge landmark dome at Greenwich Peninsula.
➕ Off map at N8 ✉ Greenwich Peninsula, SE10 ☎ Information 0870 603 2000. Vistor center 020 8305 3456. Festival information 0870 600 2000 🚇 North Greenwich (DLR) 🚤 Riverboat to Greenwich Peninsula 🎫 Pre-booked ticket only

TOWER BRIDGE MUSEUM
Opened in 1894; fine views from the museum and catwalk between the towers; engine rooms at the south bank end.
➕ K6 ✉ Tower Bridge, SE1 ☎ 020 7403 3761 ⏱ Apr–Oct: daily 10–6:30. Nov–Mar: daily 9:30–6. Last admission 75 minutes before closing. Closed Good Fri 🚇 Tower Hill 🚤 Riverboat to Tower Pier 🎫 Expensive

WATERLOO & MILLENNIUM BRIDGES
Gilbert Scott's cantilevered concrete, and Caro and Rogers' superfine span, both with great views.
Waterloo Bridge ➕ H6 ✉ WC2 🚇 Waterloo
Millennium Bridge ➕ J5–J6 ✉ EC4 🚇 Mansion House

Riverboats
On a sunny day, take the underground to Westminster and catch a riverboat up or down the Thames for the morning. Trips downstream pass Westminster, the City, and Docklands, stopping at several piers. A longer trip upstream meanders past London's villages, stopping at Putney Bridge, Kew, Richmond, and Hampton Court piers.

The Prospect of Whitby, an old riverside smugglers' pub in Wapping

FAMILY FAVORITES

Backstage tours

Going behind the scenes is great fun. In London, there are some excellent backstage tours. See how the scenery, props, and costumes are made at the National Theatre (► 79), or explore backstage at the Royal Shakespeare Company's Barbican and Pit theaters (► 79). Sports-keen kids can join tours of the MCC at Lord's (► 60 panel), Rugby Football Union Stadium at Twickenham (☎ 020 8892 2000), and Wimbledon Lawn Tennis Club (☎ 020 8944 1066). Reservations recommended for all.

BBC EXPERIENCE

Interactive exhibition and tour through the BBC's story, in which you can star, too.
🕂 F4 ⊠ Broadcasting House, Portland Place, W1 ☎ 0870 603 0304 🕓 Mon 1–4:30; Tue–Fri 9:30–4:30; Sat, Sun 9:30–5:30. Tours depart regularly up to closing time 🍴 Café 🚇 Oxford Circus 💷 Expensive; family ticket. Reservations recommended

BETHNAL GREEN MUSEUM OF CHILDHOOD

This outpost of the Victoria & Albert Museum (► 28) is an enormous train shed packed with Noah's arks, dolls, toy soldiers, puppets, and even a model circus.
🕂 M3 ⊠ Cambridge Heath Road, E2 ☎ 020 8983 5200/1 🕓 Mon–Thu, Sat 10–5:30; Sun 2:30–5:50 🍴 Café 🚇 Bethnal Green 🚉 Bethnal Green 💷 Free

BRITISH AIRWAYS LONDON EYE

A 30-minute ride on the world's tallest observation wheel.
🕂 G6 ⊠ Jubilee Gardens, SE1 ☎ As for Madame Tussaud's, below 🕓 Apr–Oct: daily 9–after dusk. Nov–Mar: daily 10–6 🍴 Café 🚇 Waterloo or Westminster 💷 Expensive

FA PREMIER LEAGUE HALL OF FAME

Homage to English soccer: its story and the dreams of its fans.
🕂 G6 ⊠ County Hall, Riverside Building, Westminster Bridge Road, SE1 ☎ 0870 8488484 🕓 Daily 10–6 🍴 Café 🚇 Westminster or Waterloo 💷 Very expensive

H.M.S. *BELFAST*

Put aside two hours to clamber up, down, and around this 1938 war cruiser, visiting the cabins, gun turrets, bridge, and boiler-room.
🕂 K6 ⊠ Morgan's Lane, Tooley Street, SE1 ☎ 020 7940 6300 🕓 Mar–Oct: daily 10–6. Nov–Feb: daily 10–5 🍴 Café 🚇 London Bridge 🚉 London Bridge 💷 Moderate; family ticket

IMAX THEATERS

London's three gargantuan screens are the Pepsi Trocadero (► 59), the Science Museum (► 27), and on the South Bank.
🕂 G6 ⊠ BFI London IMAX Cinema, 1 Charlie Chaplin Walk, South Bank, SE1 ☎ 020 7902 1234 🕓 Daily noon–8:30. Late shows Fri, Sat 🚇 Waterloo 🚉 Waterloo 💷 Moderate

LONDON BALLOON COMPANY

Enjoy a bird's eye view of London from 400 feet up in the world's largest tethered helium balloon.

Model theaters in Pollock Toy Museum (► 51)

🏠 G8 ✉ Spring Gardens, SE11 ☎ 0345 023842 🕐 Mon–Fri
10–dusk; Sat, Sun 10–midnight (weather permitting) 🚇 Vauxhall
💷 Very expensive; family ticket. Ticket valid for one year if cancelled

MADAME TUSSAUD'S
& THE LONDON PLANETARIUM

Madame Tussaud learned the art of waxworks from
her uncle; see how many people you can identify,
from Shakespeare to Madonna, and do not miss
the Spirit of London ride. The Planetarium has good
star shows and an interactive exhibition area.
🏠 E4 ✉ Marylebone Road, W1 ☎ 020 7935 6861 🕐 Apr–Sep:
daily 9–5:30; Oct–Mar: daily 10–5:30. Planetarium various timings,
phone for current details 🍴 Restaurant, café 🚇 Baker Street
💷 Very expensive; family ticket; Tussaud's/Planetarium combined
ticket. Discount tickets for Rock Circus (below) available

THE ORIGINAL LONDON SIGHTSEEING TOUR

Cruise about town on an open-top double-decker bus
whose four routes cover 80 stops (► 19); tickets and
route maps available on board.
🏠 Moves around central London ✉ Pick-up points include Victoria
Street, Haymarket, Marble Arch, Strand, Charing Cross Pier ☎ 020
8877 1722 🕐 Daily 9–5:30; departures every 15 minutes
approximately 💷 Very expensive. Ticket valid 24 hours

PEPSI TROCADERO

Segaworld, Imaginator, Virtual Glider, Funland
Bumper Cars, Lazerbowl, Virtuality, the Pepsi IMAX
3D cinema, and Drop of Fear provide a giant dream
world of rides, adventure, and interactive
experiences spread over six huge floors.
🏠 F5 ✉ Piccadilly Circus, W1 ☎ 020 7416 6020 🕐 Sun–Thu
10–midnight; Fri, Sat 10AM–1AM 🍴 Restaurant, cafés 🚇 Piccadilly
Circus 💷 Entry free. Rides expensive. Day-long Adrenalin ticket

POLLOCK TOY MUSEUM (► 51)

ROCK CIRCUS

Rock legends from Mick Jagger to Jamiroquai seem
to come alive when visitors' headphones pick up
infrared signals and play their songs.
🏠 F5 ✉ London Pavilion, Piccadilly Circus, W1 ☎ 020 7734 8025
🕐 Daily 10AM–midnight 🚇 Piccadilly Circus 💷 Very expensive;
family ticket. Discount tickets for Madame Tussaud's (above) available

SEGAWORLD

See Pepsi Trocadero, above.

TOY WORLD, HARRODS

Up on the fourth floor, this is every child's dream
outing. Plenty of toys for children to play with.
🏠 D7 ✉ Brompton Road, SW1 ☎ 020 7730 1234 🕐 Mon–Sat
10–6; Wed–Fri 10–7 🍴 Restaurants, cafés 🚇 Knightsbridge 💷 Free

Harrods—an outing in itself

London for free

London has plenty of free
activities for all ages. Several
public galleries are free (National
Gallery ► 39, National Portrait
Gallery ► 38, Tate Galleries,
free except for special
exhibitions ► 34) plus the
commercial ones (► 72). Many
museums are free (British
Museum ► 43, Wallace
Collection ► 51, Bank of
England ► 50) and music can
be enjoyed in church concerts,
pubs, and arts complexes. For
free theater, try an art auction
(► 72), a debate in Parliament
(► 36), or a BBC recording
session (☎ 020 8743 8000
and ask for ticket inquiries,
specifying radio or TV).

HIDDEN LONDON

Cricket

Anyone who watches or plays cricket should visit the MCC Museum hidden away at Lord's. The story of the game is told in pictures, cartoons, and old battered bats; the Ashes are kept here, too. It is open to ticket-holders on match days, while at other times the guided tour includes the Long Room and the beautiful new stand designed by Michael Hopkins in 1985–7.

➕ D3 ✉ Marylebone Cricket Club, Lord's Ground, NW8 ☎ 020 7289 1611. Tour bookings 020 7432 1033 🕐 Guided tours daily noon, 2; match days 10, noon, 2; major match days none 🚇 St. John's Wood 🚶 Expensive

See Top 25 Sights for BANQUETING HOUSE (➤ 37)

CHELSEA PHYSIC GARDEN
Sir Hans Sloane laid out this walled garden for the Society of Apothecaries in 1673.
➕ D8 ✉ Swan Walk, SW3 ☎ 020 7352 5646 🕐 Apr–Oct: Wed noon–5; Sun (usually) 2–6 🍴 Tea available 🚇 Sloane Square 🚶 Moderate

DULWICH PICTURE GALLERY (➤ 50)

INNER AND MIDDLE TEMPLE
These two Inns of Court are named after the Knights Templar, whose church (➤ 55) is here, too.
➕ H5 ✉ Middle Temple, Middle Temple Lane, EC4 ☎ 020 7427 4800 🕐 Middle Temple Hall Mon–Fri 10–11:30, 3–4:30 (phone first). Closed Aug and public hols 🚇 Temple 🚶 Free

ROYAL HOSPITAL, CHELSEA
Wren's 1682 building, inspired by the Hôtel des Invalides in Paris, is still a home for veteran soldiers.
➕ E8 ✉ Royal Hospital Road, SW3 ☎ 020 7730 0161 🕐 Museum, Great Hall and Chapel Mon–Fri 10–noon, 2–4; Sat 2–4. Sun service 10:40. Closed May 15–end Jun and public hols 🚇 Sloane Square 🚶 Free

ST. DUNSTAN IN THE EAST
Wren's 1698 tower soars above a secret garden.
➕ K5 ✉ St. Dunstan's Hill, EC3 🕐 Mon–Fri dawn–dusk 🚇 Monument or Tower Hill 🚶 Free

ST. ETHELDREDA'S CHAPEL (➤ 55)

ST. GEORGE, HANOVER SQUARE GARDENS
Tree-shaded oasis in Mayfair.
➕ E5 ✉ Enter from South Audley Street and Mount Street, W1 🚇 Bond Street, Green Park 🚶 Free

SUTTON HOUSE
Tudor house (1535) with linen-fold paneling and wall paintings.
➕ M1 ✉ 2 Homerton Street, E9 ☎ 020 8986 2264 🕐 Feb–Nov: Wed, Sun, public hols 11:30–5:30; Sat 2–5:30. Last admission 5PM 🍴 Café 🚇 Homerton 🚶 Inexpensive

Chelsea Pensioners, residents of the Royal Hospital, Chelsea

TEMPLE OF MITHRAS
The ground floor of this Roman temple survives, relocated to the public pavement.
➕ J5 ✉ Bucklersbury, EC4 🕐 24 hours 🚇 Bank 🚶 Free

LONDON
where to...

61

ENGLISH RESTAURANTS

Prices

Eating out in London is generally expensive and prices vary widely. In the restaurants listed on these pages, expect to pay per person for a meal (excluding drinks):

$	more than £12
$$	more than £25
$$$	more than £35

When the check arrives, look it over carefully as service charge (usually 10–12½ percent) and sometimes cover charges (approximately £1.50 per person) may be added. Check beforehand whether VAT and coffee are also included, and order tap water if you do not want to pay for bottled. A good-value menu can be transformed into an outrageous check if you do not look sharp. You are not obliged to leave a tip if service is added even if the credit card is left open.

English cuisine

English cuisine may be derided, but there is in fact both fine traditional and impressive new wave cooking to be enjoyed.

ALASTAIR LITTLE: LANCASTER ROAD ($$)

If Alastair Little's plate-glass Soho showpiece is beyond the purse, come to this less formal but highly fashionable outpost.

✚ A5 ✉ 136a Lancaster Road, W11 ☎ 020 7243 2220 ⏰ Mon–Sat lunch, dinner Ⓔ Ladbroke Grove

ATLANTIC BAR AND GRILL ($$)

Big, impressive basement in the Regent Palace Hotel off Piccadilly Circus. Good bar attracts a smart, young clientele. Dress trendily.

✚ F5 ✉ 20 Glasshouse Street, W1 ☎ 020 7734 4888 ⏰ Mon–Fri lunch; daily dinner Ⓔ Piccadilly Circus

FRENCH HOUSE DINING ROOM ($$)

Cozy dining room over a Soho pub serving modern dishes. Its Clerkenwell outpost is the St. John.

✚ F5 ✉ 45 Dean Street, W1 ☎ 020 7437 2477 ⏰ Mon–Sat lunch, dinner Ⓔ Tottenham Court Road

THE IVY ($$)

A revived theaterland classic with artworks by Peter Blake and Howard Hodgkin on the walls, celebrities galore and modern English food. Reservations essential.

✚ G5 ✉ 1 West Street, WC2 ☎ 020 7836 4751 ⏰ Lunch, dinner Ⓔ Leicester Square

J SHEEKEY ($$)

Major face-lift has revitalized one of London's oldest and best-known seafood restaurants. Traditional fish dishes alongside more modern creations.

✚ G5 ✉ 28–32 St. Martin's Court, WC2 ☎ 020 7240 2565 ⏰ Lunch, dinner Ⓔ Leicester Square

LEITH'S ($$$)

Imaginative, inventive recipes, with plenty of vegetarian dishes in a new, rather sterile interior.

✚ A5 ✉ 92 Kensington Park Road, W11 ☎ 020 7229 4481 ⏰ Tue–Fri lunch; Mon–Sat dinner Ⓔ Notting Hill Gate

RULES ($$)

One of London's oldest restaurants, founded in 1798, serves good traditional English dishes in plush Edwardian rooms.

✚ G5 ✉ 35 Maiden Lane, WC2 ☎ 020 7836 5314 ⏰ Lunch, dinner Ⓔ Covent Garden

SIMPSON'S ($$)

Opened in 1848 as Simpson's Divan and Tavern, where chess players lolled on divans to feast on roast beef. Today, there's just the roast beef and other traditional dishes. Dress code: jacket and tie.

✚ G5 ✉ 110 Strand, WC2 ☎ 020 7836 9112 ⏰ Lunch, dinner Ⓔ Aldwych

STEPHEN BULL ($$)

Stephen Bull's original, minimalist restaurant delivers robust, contemporary English/ British food. There are branches in Clerkenwell and St. Martin's Lane.

✚ E5 ✉ 7 Blandford Street, W1 ☎ 020 7486 9696 ⏰ Mon–Fri lunch; Mon–Sat dinner Ⓔ Baker Street

ITALIAN & FRENCH RESTAURANTS

AL SAN VINCENZO ($$)

It is essential to reserve a table to enjoy Neapolitan Signore Borgonzolo's cooking.

🏠 D5 ✉ 30 Connaught Street, W2 ☎ 020 7262 9623 ⏰ Mon–Fri lunch; Mon–Sat dinner 🚇 Marble Arch

ASSAGGI ($$)

Popular Italian above the Chepstow pub specializing in a dozen or so starters called *assaggi* (little tastes).

🏠 B5 ✉ The Chepstow, 39 Chepstow Place, W2 ☎ 020 7792 5501 ⏰ Lunch, dinner 🚇 Westbourne Park

BERTORELLI'S ($$)

A Covent Garden favorite. Lively atmosphere, good food, and efficient service, coping with the pre- or post-opera rush from across the way.

🏠 G5 ✉ 44a Floral Street, WC2 ☎ 020 7836 3969 ⏰ Lunch, dinner 🚇 Covent Garden

CAFÉ DU MARCHÉ ($$)

In the cobblestone mews in the square's west corner, this rustic French restaurant has a laid-back pianist each evening.

🏠 J4 ✉ 22 Charterhouse Square, EC1 ☎ 020 7608 1609 ⏰ Mon–Fri lunch; Mon–Sat dinner 🚇 Barbican

CHEZ MOI ($$)

This romantic restaurant of long standing is a Kensington favorite for reliable French cooking.

🏠 A6 ✉ 1 Addison Avenue, W11 ☎ 020 7603 8267, fax 020 7603 3898 ⏰ Mon–Fri lunch; Mon–Sat dinner 🚇 Holland Park

L'ALTRO ($$)

Fashionable Kensington establishment serving Italian seafood on earthenware platters. Much patronized by locals.

🏠 A5 ✉ 210 Kensington Park Road, W11 ☎ 020 7792 1066/1077 ⏰ Lunch, dinner 🚇 Ladbroke Grove

L'ESCARGOT ($$)

Stylish brasserie, a true Soho landmark, serving modern French cooking.

🏠 G5 ✉ 48 Greek Street, W1 ☎ 020 7437 6828, fax 020 7437 0790 ⏰ Mon–Fri lunch; Mon–Sat dinner 🚇 Leicester Square

PALAIS DU JARDIN ($$)

Congenial atmosphere and food in a huge, smart brasserie, with tables outside in summer.

🏠 G5 ✉ 136 Long Acre, WC2 ☎ 020 7379 5353 ⏰ Lunch, dinner 🚇 Leicester Square or Covent Garden

SPIGA ($)

Pizzas from a wood-fired oven form the core, but simple pasta and fish dishes are highly recommended.

🏠 F5 ✉ 84–6 Wardour Street, W1 ☎ 020 7734 3444, fax 020 7734 3332 ⏰ Lunch, dinner 🚇 Piccadilly Circus

ZAFFERANO ($$)

Giorgio Locatelli specializes in modern interpretations of simple Italian country cooking. Keen prices for a smart location.

🏠 D7 ✉ 15 Lowndes Street, SW1 ☎ 020 7235 5800, fax 020 72351971 ⏰ Mon–Sat lunch, dinner 🚇 Knightsbridge

Set-price menus

Many of London's pricier restaurants offer two set-price menus serving sublime dishes—lower in price at lunchtime. Consider dressing up to try classic Anglo-French cuisine at the exquisite Connaught Grill (🏠 E5 ✉ 16 Carlos Place, W1 ☎ 020 7499 7070) or spend an afternoon lunching at Pierre Koffman's La Tante Claire (► 66). All the star chefs offer these menus, from Alastair Little (► 62) and Gordon Ramsay to Philip Howard, Marco Pierrre White, and Michel Roux (all ► 66).

CHINESE & FAR EASTERN RESTAURANTS

Fish galore

With the increased popularity of fish, most London restaurants are cooking it better and those devoted to fish, very well. For traditional recipes try Sweetings, in the City (✉ 39 Queen Victoria Street), or Green's Restaurant & Oyster Bar (✉ 36 Duke Street, St. James's) — the English oyster season covers all the months with an 'r' in them. Less formal are L'Altro (► 63) and Livebait (✉ 43 The Cut, SE1). Less formal are L'Altro (► 63) and Livebait (✉ 43 The Cut, SE1). For a modern take on classic fish dishes try J Sheekey (► 62). For good fish and chips, try Wilton Road, behind Victoria

THE BIRDCAGE ($$)
Striking Thai-inspired setting for Michael von Hruschka's unique, ultra-modern interpretation of Far Eastern cuisine.
➕ F4 ✉ 110 Whitfield Street, W1 ☎ 020 7323 9655
🕐 Mon–Fri lunch; Mon–Sat dinner 🚇 Goodge Street

CHURCHILL ARMS ($)
London's first pub to serve tasty, inexpensive Thai food. Best to reserve.
➕ B6 ✉ 119 Kensington Church Street, W8 ☎ 020 7792 1246 🕐 Daily lunch; Mon–Sat dinner 🚇 Notting Hill Gate

FUNG SHING ($$)
Consistently good Cantonese dishes—follow the manager's advice.
➕ G5 ✉ 15 Lisle Street, WC2 ☎ 020 7437 1539 🕐 Lunch, dinner 🚇 Leicester Square

HARBOUR CITY ($)
Great *dim sum* in a highly reputed Soho Chinese restaurant.
➕ G5 ✉ 46 Gerrard Street, W1 ☎ 020 7439 7859
🕐 Lunch, dinner 🚇 Leicester Square

IMPERIAL CITY ($$)
Accomplished Chinese cooking served in the Royal Exchange vaults.
➕ K5 ✉ Royal Exchange, Cornhill, EC3 ☎ 020 7626 3437 🕐 Mon–Fri lunch, dinner 🚇 Bank

NOBU ($$$)
New York's Nobuyuki Matsuhisa brings his pan-American Japanese cooking to the cool Metropolitan Hotel.
➕ E6 ✉ Metropolitan Hotel, 19 Old Park Lane, W1 ☎ 020 7447 4747, fax 020 7447 4749

🕐 Mon–Fri lunch; daily dinner Sat, Sun 🚇 Hyde Park Corner

ROYAL CHINA ($$)
Reserve a table or join the justifiably long lines for the best *dim sum* in town.
➕ C5 ✉ 13 Queensway, W2 ☎ 020 7221 2535 🕐 Lunch, dinner. No reservations necessary Sat, Sun 🚇 Queensway

SINGAPORE GARDEN ($$)
Favorite with north Londoners for its Malaysian and Indonesian seasonal specialties. Always packed. Branch in Gloucester Place.
➕ C2 ✉ 83–83a Fairfax Road, NW6 ☎ 020 7328 5314 🕐 Lunch, dinner 🚇 Swiss Cottage

TUI ($$)
Simple but popular Thai restaurant; convenient for South Kensington museums.
➕ D7 ✉ 19 Exhibition Road, SW7 ☎ 020 7584 8359 🕐 Lunch, dinner 🚇 South Kensington

VONG ($$$)
Jean-Georges Vongerichten—from Alsace via New York—fuses French and Thai cuisines.
➕ E6 ✉ The Berkeley Hotel, Wilton Place, SW1 ☎ 020 7235 1010 🕐 Mon–Sat lunch, dinner 🚇 Hyde Park Corner

WAGAMAMA ($)
Trendy Japanese *ramen* bar near the British Museum. Branch in Lexington Street, W1.
➕ G5 ✉ 4 Streatham Street, WC1 ☎ 020 7323 9223 🕐 Lunch, dinner 🚇 Tottenham Court Road

INDIAN & VEGETARIAN RESTAURANTS

CAFÉ SPICE NAMASTE ($)

Cyrus Todiwala's agreeable food in a jolly setting. Near the Tower of London. Lunch reservations essential.

📍 L5 ✉ 16 Prescot Street, E1 ☎ 020 7488 9242 🕐 Mon–Fri lunch; Mon–Sat dinner 🚇 Aldgate

CHOR BIZARRE ($$)

Crowded Indian "thieves market" seating. Some unusual regional dishes among the tandooris and thalis.

📍 F6 ✉ 16 Albemarle Street, W1 ☎ 020 7629 9802, fax 020 7493 7756 🕐 Lunch, dinner 🚇 Green Park

CRANKS ($)

The mother of London veggie restaurants and one of a chain serving good-value, quality food. Covent Garden and Great Newport Street branches are open Sundays.

📍 F5 ✉ 8 Marshall Street, W1 ☎ 020 7437 9431 🕐 Mon–Sat 8–8 breakfast, lunch, dinner 🚇 Oxford Circus

DIWANA BHEL POORI HOUSE ($)

Bhel poori are fried snacks sold on Bombay streets and beaches; in this vegetarian restaurant they are served as first courses.

📍 F4 ✉ 121 Drummond Street, NW1 ☎ 020 7387 5556 🕐 Lunch buffet, dinner (bring your own alcohol) 🚇 Euston

THE OLD DELHI ($$)

Rich north Indian dishes laced with memories of their Persion origins. Some purely Persion dishes, too.

📍 D5 ✉ 48 Kendal Street, W2

☎ 020 7723 3335 🕐 Lunch, dinner 🚇 Marble Arch

RASA W1 ($$)

Das Shreedharan's inspired Keralan vegetarian dishes is a brilliant introduction to this regional cuisine.

📍 E5 ✉ 6 Dering Street, W1 ☎ 020 7629 1346 🕐 Lunch, dinner 🚇 Oxford Circus

SALLOOS ($$)

Upscale, authentic northwest frontier food for meateaters, cooked by Mr Salahuddin of Lahore.

📍 E6 ✉ 62–4 Kinnerton Street, SW1 ☎ 020 7235 4444 🕐 Mon–Sat lunch, dinner 🚇 Hyde Park Corner

TAMARIND ($$)

Traditional dishes by Atul Kochhar from villages in Uttar Pradesh to Kerala.

📍 E6 ✉ 20 Queen Street, W1 ☎ 020 7629 3561 🕐 Sun–Fri lunch; daily dinner 🚇 Green Park

VEERASWAMY ($$)

London's oldest Indian restaurant brought up to date with a complete make over. Classical Indian food with a modern twist to suit Western palates. Same owners as the better-known Chutney Mary at 535 King's Road.

📍 F5 ✉ 99 Regent Street, W1 ☎ 020 7734 1401 🕐 Lunch, dinner 🚇 Piccadilly Circus

WORLD FOOD CAFÉ ($)

A fresh, modern approach to vegetarian food, with Indian, Mexican, Greek, and Turkish influences.

📍 G5 ✉ 14 Neal's Yard, WC2 ☎ 020 7379 0298 🕐 Mon–Sat noon–5pm 🚇 Covent Garden

Indian food

An Indian meal should have many dishes so if you are a group, consider making a collective order and sharing. Tandoori dishes (cooked in a clay oven) make good starters. Main course dishes should arrive together and include one or two meat offerings, two or three vegetable dishes, rice, a lentil or pulse serving (such as chickpeas), and a variety of breads such as *chapati* or *naan*—which are eaten hot, so order more as you go along. Remember the yogurt and pickles, and drink *lassi* (sweet or salty variations on buttermilk/yogurt) or beer. Vegetarians will find a good range of mild and spicy food in London's 2,000 Indian restaurants.

FAMOUS CHEFS

RICHARD CORRIGAN: LINDSAY HOUSE ($$)
Inspired modern British cooking from one of London's top chefs.
🔛 G5 ✉ 21 Romilly Street, W1 ☎ 020 7439 0450 🕐 Mon–Fri lunch; Mon–Sat dinner 🚇 Piccadilly Circus

PHILIP HOWARD: THE SQUARE ($$)
Impressive food matched by a chic, contemporary interior and Bond Street swank.
🔛 F5 ✉ 6 Bruton Street, W1 ☎ 020 7495 7100 🕐 Mon–Fri lunch; Mon–Sat dinner 🚇 Bond Street

PIERRE KOFFMANN: LA TANTE CLAIRE, THE BERKELEY HOTEL ($$$)
One of London's best French chefs explores the cuisine of his native Gascony. New location.
🔛 E6 ✉ The Berkeley Hotel, Wilton Place, SW1 ☎ 020 7823 2003 🕐 Mon–Fri lunch, dinner 🚇 Hyde Park Corner

NICO LADENIS: CHEZ NICO AT 90 PARK LANE ($$$)
Sheer skill and powerful flavors drive this great man's ideas.
🔛 E5 ✉ Grosvenor House Hotel, 90 Park Lane, W1 ☎ 020 7409 1290, fax 020 7355 4877 🕐 Mon–Fri lunch, dinner 🚇 Marble Arch

JEAN-CHRISTOPHE NOVELLI: MAISON NOVELLI ($$$)
Well worth bypassing the brasserie for the pricier upstairs restaurant.
🔛 H4 ✉ 29 Clerkenwell Green, EC1 ☎ 020 7251 6606 🕐 Mon–Fri lunch, dinner 🚇 Farringdon

GORDON RAMSAY: GORDON RAMSAY RESTAURANT ($$$)
Advance reservations are required if you want to sample a breathtaking interpretation of French cooking.
🔛 E8 ✉ 68 Royal Hospital Road, SW3 ☎ 020 7352 4441 🕐 Mon–Fri lunch, dinner 🚇 Sloane Square

RUTH ROGERS AND ROSE GRAY: RIVER CAFÉ ($$$)
Outstanding modern Italian food in Richard Rogers's striking setting (▶ 9).
🔛 Off map at A8 ✉ Thames Wharf, Rainville Road, W6 ☎ 020 7381 8824 🕐 Daily lunch; Mon–Sat dinner 🚇 Hammersmith

MICHEL ROUX: LA GAVROCHE ($$$)
Albert's son sticks to classic French, but lighter.
🔛 E5 ✉ 43 Upper Brook Street, W1 ☎ 020 7408 0881 🕐 Mon–Sat lunch, dinner 🚇 Oxford Circus

MARCO PIERRE WHITE: THE OAK ROOM ($$$)
Opulent surroundings for cooking that is the ultimate in luxury and perfection. Marco Pierre White continues to outflank his culinary rivals.
🔛 F5 ✉ Le Meridien Piccadilly, 21 Piccadilly W1 ☎ 020 7437 0202 🕐 Mon–Fri lunch; Mon–Sat dinner 🚇 Piccadilly Circus

Riverside eating
London is exploiting the potential of its riverside views. Today, there is more than just the grand Savoy River Room (▶ 67) and the East End smugglers' pubs. The most spectacular views are from the Oxo Tower Restaurant (✉ Barge House Street, SE1) with its serious food— and prices—as well as the Tate Gallery of Modern Art's rooftop restaurant at Bankside (▶ 34 and 54). There are lower but impressive views from the second-floor Blue Print Café, beside the Design Museum, Butler's Wharf, overlooking Tower Bridge and the City (▶ 50). For more modest river-view eating, try Barley Mow pub (✉ 44 Narrow Street, E14), whose outdoor tables overlook the wider, curving Thames of the East End.

BREAKFAST & TEA

CAFÉ DE PARIS ($)

The Pyramid Tea Dance is the real thing: ballroom and Latin dancing classics plus full afternoon tea. Dress code: dancing.

✚ G5 ✉ 3 Coventry Street, W1 ☎ 020 7734 7700
◉ Sun tea 🚇 Piccadilly Circus

CLARIDGE'S ($$)

Breakfast is in the immaculate art deco restaurant; tea—among the best in London—is taken on sofas in the lobby alcove. Reservations essential. Dress code: jacket and tie.

✚ E5 ✉ Brook Street, W1 ☎ 020 7629 8860
◉ Breakfast, tea 🚇 Bond Street

COFFEE GALLERY ($)

Italian-run café, ideal for pre-museum coffee and croissants, and post-museum pasta and cakes.

✚ G5 ✉ 23 Museum Street, WC1 ☎ 020 7436 0455
◉ Mon–Sat breakfast, tea
🚇 Leicester Square

FOUNDATION AT HARVEY NICHOLS ($$)

Chic, cool basement, as design-aware as the five floors of fashion above it.

✚ E6 ✉ Knightsbridge (Saville Street entrance), SW1 ☎ 020 7201 8000
◉ Breakfast, lunch, tea
🚇 Knightsbridge

BLISS ($)

Sumptuous croissants, quiches, and feather-light *tartes au citron*, ideal pre- or post-Camden Passage (antiques).

✚ H3 ✉ 428 St. John Street, EC1 ☎ 020 7837 3720
◉ Mon–Sat 8–6; Sun 9–5
🚇 Angel

MANDARIN ORIENTAL HYDE PARK ($$)

The window tables in the lounge conservatory overlooking Hyde Park are the best for afternoon tea.

✚ E6 ✉ Knightsbridge, SW1 ☎ 020 7235 2000
◉ Breakfast, tea 🚇 Hyde Park Corner

PÂTISSERIE VALERIE ($)

Coffee, croissants, and delicious cakes at tiny tables in the original café-shop. Six branches.

✚ F5 ✉ 44 Old Compton Street, W1 ☎ 020 7437 3466
◉ Breakfast, tea 🚇 Leicester Square or Tottenham Court Road

SAVOY HOTEL ($$)

Reserve a window table for breakfast in the River Room; tea is on sofas in the pretty Thames Foyer. Dress code: jacket and tie.

✚ G5 ✉ Strand, WC2 ☎ 020 7836 4343
◉ Breakfast, tea 🚇 Aldwych

SIMPSON'S ($$)

Glorious setting for a traditional breakfast, such as porridge followed by kippers or kidneys. Dress code: jacket and tie.

✚ G5 ✉ 100 Strand, WC2 ☎ 020 7836 9112
◉ Breakfast, tea 🚇 Aldwych

LE MERIDIEN WALDORF ($$)

Buffet-style breakfast in the lofty Palm Court; tea is traditional, with weekend tea dances (for which a jacket and tie is required).

✚ G5 ✉ Aldwych, WC2 ☎ 020 7836 2400
◉ Breakfast, tea 🚇 Aldwych

Best settings

If part of the pleasure of dining out is the setting, try the Ritz (► 84) at lunchtime for grandeur; the mosaic-clad Criterion (✉ 224 Piccadilly, W1) for sparkle; Claridge's (► 84) for art deco, and the Café Royal (✉ Regent Street, W1) for *fin de siècle*. Wacky settings include the Dorchester's pricey Oriental (✉ Park Lane, W1). For atmospheric pubs, go to the George Inn (✉ 77 Borough High Street, SE1); the River Café (► 66) or Oxo Tower Restaurant (✉ Barge House Street, SE1) are architects' dreams. And you'll find the most beautiful walls at Christopher's (► 68).

BRASSERIES & BRUNCH

The American experience

America's fast food arrived long before its quality cuisine and restaurant style became established. Upscale options include Joe Allen and Christopher's (both this page), and PJ's Grill (✉ 52 Fulham Road, SW3). Other good-value places to hang out include:

The Hard Rock Café
✉ 150 Old Park Lane, W1

Kenny's
✉ 2a Pond Place, SW3

Rock Island Diner
✉ Plaza Centre, London Pavilion, Piccadilly

Planet Hollywood
✉ Trocadero Centre, Coventry Street, W1

Fatboy's Diner
✉ 21 Maiden Lane, WC2

Chicago Pizza Pie Factory
✉ 17 Hanover Square, W1

TGIF
✉ 6 Bedford Street (and branches)

BRASSERIE DU MARCHÉ AUX PUCES ($$)

At the north end of Portobello Road; ideal after Portobello Market.
🚇 B5 ✉ 349 Portobello Road, W10 ☎ 020 8968 5828
🕐 Breakfast, lunch, dinner
🚇 Ladbroke Grove

LA BRASSERIE ST. QUENTIN ($$)

Uncompromisingly French—great for an indulgent break from a South Kensington Museums day.
🚇 D7 ✉ 243 Brompton Road, SW3 ☎ 020 7589 8005
🕐 Lunch, dinner 🚇 South Kensington

CAMDEN BRASSERIE ($$)

Good for grilled steak, *frites*, and a bottle of wine after Camden Lock markets.
🚇 F2 ✉ 214–16 Camden High Street, NW1 ☎ 020 7482 2114 🕐 Lunch, dinner; Sun brunch 🚇 Camden Town

CHRISTOPHER'S ($$)

One of the best London haunts for a genuine American brunch, and in one of the capital's most beautiful dining rooms.
🚇 G5 ✉ 18 Wellington Street, WC2 ☎ 020 7240 4222
🕐 Lunch, dinner; Sat, Sun brunch 🚇 Aldwych or Covent Garden

DAKOTA ($$)

U.S. southwestern cooking that's a hit with A-list celebs and cool locals.
🚇 B5 ✉ 127 Ledbury Road, W11 ☎ 020 7792 9191
🕐 Lunch, dinner 🚇 Notting Hill Gate

JOE ALLEN ($$)

Dependably convivial and club-like. Healthy American Cal-Ital food served by smiling waiters. Reservations essential.
🚇 G5 ✉ 13 Exeter Street, WC2 ☎ 020 7836 0651
🕐 Lunch, dinner; Sat, Sun brunch 🚇 Covent Garden

JUSTIN DE BLANK ($)

Modern brasserie with easygoing charm. Saturday brunch is recommended.
🚇 E4 ✉ 120 Marylebone High Street, W1 ☎ 020 7361 1910 🕐 Mon–Sat lunch, dinner 🚇 Bond Street

MASH ($$)

Bar/restaurant/micro brewery rolled into one. Wide-ranging menu with imaginative pizzas, weekend brunch, and lots of global influences.
🚇 F4 ✉ 19–21 Great Portland Street, W1 ☎ 020 7637 5555 🕐 Breakfast, lunch, dinner 🚇 Oxford Circus

MEZZONINE ($$)

One of the largest bar/restaurants in Europe serving Med/Asian food. But it's the barmen who are superb and outstrip the chefs. An experience.
🚇 F5 ✉ 100 Wardour Street, W1 ☎ 020 7314 4000
🕐 Lunch, dinner 🚇 Piccadilly Circus

UNION CAFE & RESTAURANT ($$)

Stylish, casual, very popular, where simple ideas are translated into fresh, appealing food.
🚇 E4 ✉ 96 Marylebone Lane, W1 ☎ 020 7486 4860
🕐 Mon–Sat breakfast, lunch, tea, dinner 🚇 Bond Street

SHOPS & PUBS

ABINGDON ($$)

Corner pub in a smart residential Kensington street that's been transformed into an airy bistro with light modern cooking.

🞡 B7 ✉ 54 Abingdon Road, W8 ☎ 020 7937 3339 🕙 Lunch, dinner 🚇 High Street Kensington

DUKE OF YORK ($)

Lunch is understandably packed in this dated, well-worn pub with its excellent Mediterranean-inspired food.

🞡 G4 ✉ 7 Roger Street, WC1 ☎ 020 7242 7230 🕙 Lunch, dinner 🚇 Russell Square

THE EAGLE ($)

The first of London's new-wave pubs (opened 1991) serves robust, Mediterranean food to a noisy, full house.

🞡 H4 ✉ 159 Farringdon Road, EC1 ☎ 020 7837 1353 🕙 Mon–Sat lunch, dinner 🚇 Farringdon

FIFTH FLOOR AT HARVEY NICHOLS ($$)

Henry Harris cooks modern British cuisine for a chic clientele in Julian Wickham's designer room. As an alternative, try the *Fountain* in the basement.

🞡 E6 ✉ Knightsbridge, SW1 ☎ 020 7235 5250 🕙 Daily lunch; Mon–Sat dinner 🚇 Knightsbridge

HARRODS ($–$$)

With 19 eateries swinging into action each day, you are spoilt for choice. Favorites include the Health Juice Bar in the basement; the Champagne and Oyster Bar, Café Espresso and Bar à Fromage (first floor); the Georgian Restaurant and Terrace Bar (good for afternoon tea, fifth floor); the Ice cream Parlor and Upper Circle Self-Service.

🞡 D7 ✉ Knightsbridge, SW1 ☎ 020 7730 1234 🕙 Breakfast, lunch, tea 🚇 Knightsbridge

LAMB TAVERN ($)

Regulars claim this restored Victorian pub in Leadenhall Market serves the best hot roast beef sandwiches in the City.

🞡 K5 ✉ 10–12 Leadenhall Market, EC3 ☎ 020 7626 2454 🕙 Mon–Fri lunch 🚇 Bank or Monument

NICOLE'S ($$)

Basement of Nicole Farhi's designer store. Expect some sensational ideas and flavors.

🞡 F5 ✉ 158 New Bond Street, W1 ☎ 020 7499 8408 🕙 Mon–Fri lunch; Mon–Sat dinner 🚇 Bond Street

PEASANT ($)

Excellent innovative Italian food in a pub touched with the wand of a design-conscious foodie.

🞡 H4 ✉ 240 St. John Street, EC1 ☎ 020 7336 7726 🕙 Mon–Fri lunch; Mon–Sat dinner 🚇 Farringdon

SOTHEBY'S ($$)

The lobby of this auction house is great for a light lunch (for which reservations are essential) or afternoon tea.

🞡 B7 ✉ 34 Bond Street, W1 ☎ 020 7293 5077 🕙 Mon–Fri breakfast, lunch, tea 🚇 Bond Street

Museum restaurants

Hugely improved, the best are the restaurants in the Tate Galleries (➤ 34 and 54), the Blue Print above the Design Museum (➤ 50), and the simpler National Gallery's Brasserie (➤ 39) overlooking Trafalgar Square, and its basement café. The Royal Academy's restaurant is decorated by Academicians (➤ 51). Kensington Palace's magnificent Orangery (➤ 25) offers the ultimate tea and the Courtauld Gallery's tiny café provides delicious soups (➤ 41).

Eat as much as you can buffet deals

Unlimited food at a fixed price is practical for families with growing children—or simply for hungry adults. Le Meridien Waldorf Hotel's buffet breakfast makes a hearty start to the day (➤ 67). Many larger hotels, such as Basil Street (➤ 85), do the equivalent at lunchtime. Sunday lunch buffets in Indian restaurants are fun.

Shopping Areas

Opening times

Regular store hours are 9:30 or 10AM until between 5:30 and 7PM, with late-night shopping in Knightsbridge on Wednesdays and Oxford Street, Regent Street, and Covent Garden on Thursdays. London's stores tend to be found in clusters; conserve your energy and shop in one area.

Tax-free goods

If you are a non-E.U. passport holder, consider the VAT Retails Export Scheme. VAT (Value Added Tax) is rated at 17½ percent in Britain and payable on almost everything except books, food, and children's clothes. All non-E.U. passport holders are exempt from VAT if they are taking the goods out of the country within three months. The tax must be paid first, then claimed back. You must have your passport and return ticket with you; the shop assistant will help you complete the form VAT407—make sure you keep your part of it along with the export sales bill. Show Customs this form and have your goods ready to show.

BOND STREET

Bond Street mixes haute couture outlets with art galleries. Asprey's, one of the world's great luxury stores, is here, as are the Fine Art Society and Sotheby's.

➕ F5 ✉ Mayfair, W1 ⊜ Bond Street or Green Park

BROMPTON CROSS

Sophisticated fashion and design stores. The Conran Shop, selling quality design furniture, is the longest-established retailer.

➕ D7 ✉ Knightsbridge/ Chelsea, SW3 ⊜ Knightsbridge or South Kensington

JERMYN STREET

Once the local street for aristocrats swarming around St. James's Palace; the atmosphere on Jermyn Street remains select: Floris the perfumier (est. 1730); Paxton & Whitfield for cheeses; and Harvie & Hudson or Turnbull & Asser for shirts.

➕ F6 ✉ St. James's, SW1 ⊜ Piccadilly Circus or Green Park

KENSINGTON CHURCH STREET

This once-quiet lane now has more than 50 antiques stores, Clarke's restaurant bakery, and Kensington Place.

➕ B6 ✉ Kensington, W8 ⊜ Notting Hill Gate or High Steet Kensington

NEAL STREET

The epitome of Covent Garden's successful rebirth, this pedestrian street is packed with exotic little stores: Smith's Gallery, the Kite Shop and, in Neal's Yard, a feast of wholefoods.

➕ G5 ✉ Covent Garden, WC2 ⊜ Covent Garden

OLD COMPTON STREET

In the 18th century, this was the social center for French exiles. Pâtisserie Valerie at No. 44 (▶ 67) keeps the mood alive; Italians run the tiny Pollo and Presto bars, Vinorio, Camisa, and the newsstand Moroni's.

➕ F5 ✉ Soho, W1 ⊜ Tottenham Court Road

OXFORD STREET

The capital's main shopping artery. At the west end, Marks & Spencer stocks the chain's greatest variety of clothing; in the middle the revamped Selfridges & Co, and branches of all significant chains from Body Shop to Gap and John Lewis.

➕ E5–G5 ✉ Mayfair/ Marylebone, W1 ⊜ Oxford Circus, Bond Street, Marble Arch, Tottenham Court Road

REGENT STREET

With its dramatic curve north from Piccadilly, John Nash's street is as smart as intended: Tower Records, Austin Reed, the sumptuous Café Royal, Mappin & Webb (silver), Garrard (jewels), Hamleys (toys), Liberty (▶ 71), and the Warner Bros and Disney stores. North of Oxford Street lies the excellent BBC store.

➕ F5 ✉ Mayfair/Soho, W1 ⊜ Piccadilly Circus or Oxford Street

DEPARTMENT STORES

FORTNUM & MASON
Before going in, do not miss the clock, which has Messrs. Fortnum and Mason mincing forward each hour. Prices are high, but the store-brand goods make perfect presents.
➕ F6 ✉ 181 Piccadilly, W1
☎ 020 7734 8040
🚇 Piccadilly Circus or Green Park

GENERAL TRADING COMPANY
Chic, small-scale department store with quality buys in all areas from china to gardening. Excellent mail-order catalog.
➕ E7 ✉ 144 Sloane Street, SW1 ☎ 020 7730 0411
🚇 Sloane Square

HARRODS
This vast emporium contains just about everything anyone could want, and 19 places to eat. Apart from the revamped fashion departments, do not miss the spectacular food halls.
➕ D6 ✉ Knightsbridge, SW1
☎ 020 7730 1234
🚇 Knightsbridge

HARVEY NICHOLS
London's classiest clothes store, from its original storefront window displays to the well-stocked fashion floors.
➕ E6 ✉ 109–25 Knightsbridge, SW1 ☎ 020 7235 5000 🚇 Knightsbridge

JOHN LEWIS
Its slogan, "never knowingly undersold," inspires a confidence that prices are solidly fair.
➕ F5 ✉ Oxford Street, W1
☎ 020 7629 7711 🚇 Oxford Circus

LIBERTY
Offering everything from sumptuous fabrics to china and glass, this store's quality is characterized by exoticism and cutting-edge fashion mixed with an Arts and Crafts heritage.
➕ F5 ✉ Regent Street, W1
☎ 020 7734 1234 🚇 Oxford Circus

MARKS & SPENCER
Most people buy something at M&S. Clothes now have sharper styles, and the food departments offer an exceptional range of pre-prepared meals.
➕ E5 ✉ 458 Oxford Street, W1 ☎ 020 7935 7954
🚇 Marble Arch

SCOTCH HOUSE
Plaid and more plaid on three floors. Especially good for soft lambswool and cashmere woolens, as well as traditional, quality Scottish clothing.
➕ D6 ✉ 2 Brompton Road, SW1 ☎ 020 7581 2151
🚇 South Kensington

SELFRIDGES & CO
This vast, bedazzling store stocks beauty products, designer labels, china, glass, and electrical goods. The food hall is worth exploring. The Christmas window displays deserve a special night outing.
➕ E5 ✉ 400 Oxford Street, W1 ☎ 020 7629 1234
🚇 Marble Arch or Bond Street

One-stop shopping
The one-stop shopping that department stores offer has several advantages over schlepping around the streets. If it rains, you stay dry. If you are hungry, there are cafés. There are also the services to be considered. Your purchases from various departments can be held for you while you shop, to be collected together at the end. Garments can be altered, presents wrapped, and writing paper printed. And most stores have dependable after-sales service if something is not right.

Street Markets

Fashion

To buy international high fashion, explore Harvey Nichols (► 71) and the stores lining Sloane Street, Brompton Cross, Beauchamp Place, Bond Street, South Molton Street, and St. Christopher's Place. For more dramatic, innovative, streetwise fashion, explore Kensington Market (✉ Kensington High Street, W8), then visit Vivienne Westwood (✉ 6 Davies Street, W1), American Retro (✉ 35 Old Compton Street, W1) and, in Covent Garden, Michiko Koshino (✉ 70 Neal Street, WC2), Jones (✉ 13 Floral Street, WC2), Space NK (✉ 41 Earlham Street, WC2), Sign of the Times (✉ Shorts Gardens, WC2), and Red or Dead (✉ 33 Neal Street, WC2).

Smithfield meat market

Smithfields (EC1) is the only large, fresh-food, commercial market left in central London. Thousands of bloody carcasses hung up on iron hooks are traded in Horace Jones's grand 19th-century building. Trading starts at 5AM and the market closes down at noon (Mon–Fri).

BERMONDSEY (NEW CALEDONIAN MARKET)

You need to know your stuff here—and, as the big dealers and auction-house experts get here before dawn, the earlier you go the better.

➕ L7 ✉ Long Lane and Bermondsey Street, SE1 🕐 Fri 5–2 🚇 Borough or London Bridge

BRIXTON MARKET

Best to go on Saturday, when the streets buzz with local African and Caribbean community shoppers buying their mangoes, sweet potatoes, snapper fish, calf's feet, and ready-cooked delicacies.

➕ Off map at H10 ✉ Brixton Station Road, Electric Avenue, and Popes Road, SW9 🕐 Mon–Wed, Fri, Sat 8–6; Thu 8–1 🚇 Brixton 🚉 Brixton

CAMDEN MARKETS

The small, vibrant market in Camden Lock has expanded and spawned other markets to fill every patch of space from the underground station up to Hawley Road. Find crafts, clothes, books and more etc.

➕ E2 ✉ Camden High Street to Chalk Farm Road, NW1 🕐 Sat, Sun 8–6 🚇 Camden Town

CAMDEN PASSAGE

Bargain at the large, twice-weekly open-air antiques market held in front of the antiques stores; then try Chapel Street market across Upper Street.

➕ H3 ✉ Islington, N1 🕐 Wed 9–mid-afternoon; Sat 9–5 🚇 Angel

GREENWICH MARKET

Hundreds of stands selling antiques and crafts, clothes, old books and more. A good start to a Greenwich day (► 20).

✉ College Approach, Stockwell Street and corner of High Road and Royal Hill, SE10 🕐 Sat, Sun 9–6 🚉 Greenwich or Island Gardens DLR then walk through the tunnel

LEADENHALL MARKET

A surprising City treat housed under Horace Jones's 1880s arcades, with quality butchers, cheesemongers, fish-mongers, and pubs.

➕ K5 ✉ Leadenhall, EC3 🕐 Mon–Fri 8–4 🚇 Bank or Monument

PETTICOAT LANE MARKET

Originally a Tudor clothes market; Jewish immigration stimulated its growth into Victorian London's largest market. Bargain hard for fashion, leather, household goods, and knickknacks. Brick Lane market is nearby.

➕ K5 ✉ Middlesex Street, E1 🕐 Sun 9–2 🚇 Aldgate or Aldgate East

PORTOBELLO MARKET

Saturday is the big day, when antiques and not-so-antiques are sold from the stores and the solid line of vendors in front of them. There are lower prices further down the hill, with second-hand stands beneath Westway.

➕ B5 ✉ Portobello Road, W11 🕐 Fruit and vegetables Mon–Sat. General Fri 8–3. Antiques Sat 8–5 🚇 Ladbroke Grove

ART & ANTIQUES

ANTIQUARIUS
London's oldest antiques center houses 120 dealers whose goods include lace, old clothes and jewelry; there are plenty of quirky, affordable items here.
🕂 D8 ✉ 131–41 King's Road, SW3 ☎ 020 7351 5353 Ⓢ Sloane Square

BONHAM'S
The strength of this auction house (still a family firm) lies in its 20th-century and specialist sales. Less expensive goods are sold in its Chelsea Galleries.
🕂 D7 ✉ Montpelier Galleries, Montpelier Street, SW7 ☎ 020 7393 3900 Ⓢ Knightsbridge

CHRISTIE'S
The auction house has departments ranging from grand old masters to coins and tribal art. A second, less expensive sale room is in South Kensington.
🕂 F6 ✉ Christie, Manson & Wood, 8 King Street, SW1 ☎ 020 7839 9060 Ⓢ Green Park

GRAY'S ANTIQUE MARKET
High-quality goods ranging from pictures to silver are sold at 170 stands.
🕂 E5 ✉ 1–7 Davies Mews and 58 Davies Street, W1 ☎ 020 7629 7034 Ⓢ Bond Street

LOTS ROAD CHELSEA AUCTION GALLERIES
Eclectic mix of antique, reproduction, and good contemporary designer furniture.
🕂 C9 ✉ 71–4 Lots Road, SW10 ☎ 020 7351 7771 Ⓢ Sloane Square then it's a 20-minute walk or bus No. 19 or 22

SOTHEBY'S
The world's largest auction house. This is a rabbit warren of sale rooms with objects of all kinds on display. The "Colonnade" sales are less expensive.
🕂 F5 ✉ 34 New Bond Street, W1 ☎ 020 7493 8080 Ⓢ Bond Street

SPINK-LEGER PICTURES
Top English paintings by artists such as Turner and Gainsborough; Agnew's, Colnaghi, Frost & Reed and Philip Mould nearby are also worth visiting.
🕂 F6 ✉ 13 Old Bond Street, W1 ☎ 020 7629 3538 Ⓢ Green Park

SPINK & SON
Best known for their coins, medals, and ravishing silver and watercolors; see also their Indian and Far Eastern department.
🕂 F6 ✉ 5 King Street, SW1 ☎ 020 7930 7888 Ⓢ Green Park

WADDINGTON GALLERIES
In a small street lined with about 20 galleries selling modern art, Waddington is just one worth seeing; try also Theo Waddington, Redfern, The Gallery, and Browse & Darby. Also worth exploring are Clifford and Derring Streets nearby.
🕂 F5 ✉ 12 and 34 Cork Street, W1 ☎ 020 7437 8611/020 439 6262 Ⓢ Green Park

Buying at auction
Watching an auction is one thing; buying is quite another. At the pre-sale viewing, inspect any lot you may bid for and check its description and estimated sale price in the catalog. If you cannot attend the sale, leave a bid; if you can, decide on your maximum bid and do not go above it! Bid by lifting your hand up high. If successful, pay and collect after the sale, or arrange for delivery.

Private galleries
An indispensible tool for visitors getting to grips with commercial art galleries in London is the monthly *Galleries* magazine, available free from most galleries. With its maps and specialist subject index, information can be called up by area as well as by subject.

BOOKS, NEW & OLD

Bookshops & cafés

To browse in a bookstore with its own in-house café, try Borders Books, Music and Cafe (✉ 203 Oxford Street, W1 ☎ 020 7292 1600 🚇 Mon–Sat 8AM–11PM, Sun noon–6 🚇 Oxford Circus). Central London branches of Books Etc with cafés include those on Charing Cross Road, Oxford Street and Piccadilly. Waterstone's superstore on Piccadilly has a café, juice bar, and restaurant.

Electronic bargains

To Europeans, London prices for electrical goods seem good value; to Americans they seem expensive. If you know what you want, compare prices up and down Tottenham Court Road for stereos, and look there as well as New Oxford Street for computers. Micro Anvika, on Tottenham Court Road, is good for hardware, software, and CD-ROMs. If daunted, go to Selfridges or Harrods (➤ 71).

BERNARD QUARITCH
It is best to make an appointment to come to this, the most splendid and serious of the city's antiquarian bookstores.
➕ F5 ✉ 5 Lower John Street, W1 ☎ 020 7734 2983 🚇 Piccadilly Circus

BOOKS FOR COOKS
Possibly the world's best selection of books about cooking and cuisine; orders are taken and dispatched worldwide.
➕ A5 ✉ 4 Blenheim Crescent, W11 ☎ 020 7221 1992 🚇 Ladbroke Grove

CINEMA BOOKSHOP
London's greatest selection of books on the movies ever. Well–informed staff, plus mail order.
➕ G5 ✉ 13–14 Great Russell Street, WC1 ☎ 020 7637 0206 🚇 Tottenham Court Road

DAUNT BOOKS
In his paneled and stained-glass elegant 1910 shop, James Daunt keeps an impressive stock of travelogs and guides.
➕ E4 ✉ 83 Marylebone High Street, NW1 ☎ 020 7224 2295 🚇 Baker Street

EDWARD STANFORD
London's largest selection of maps of countries, cities, and even very small towns around the world, together with travel books.
➕ G5 ✉ 12–14 Long Acre, WC2 ☎ 020 7836 1321 🚇 Covent Garden

FORBIDDEN PLANET
An amazing selection of fantasy, horror, science fiction; plus comic books.
➕ G5 ✉ 71–3 New Oxford Street, W1 ☎ 020 7836 4179 🚇 Tottenham Court Road

HATCHARDS
Opened in 1797; past patrons have included British army commander, the Duke of Wellington (1769–1852) and four-time prime minister William Gladstone (1809–98). With their well-informed staff, Hatchards still knows how to make book buying a delicious experience.
➕ F6 ✉ 187 Piccadilly, W1 ☎ 020 7493 9921 🚇 Piccadilly Circus

MAGGS BROTHERS
Make your appointment, then step into this Mayfair mansion to find an out-of-print book, a first edition or rare antiquarian book.
➕ E6 ✉ 50 Berkeley Square, W1 ☎ 020 7493 7160 🚇 Green Park

WATERSTONE'S
One of London's most extensive bookstore chains with many smaller branches around the capital. Good search service.
➕ F4 ✉ 82 Gower Street, WC1 ☎ 020 7636 1577 🚇 Goodge Street

ZWEMMER ARTS BOOKSHOP
Art books fill three neighboring bookstores, divided by category. Here, fine art is upstairs, decorative art and architecture downstairs. Photography and media at 80 Charing Cross Road; East European titles at 28 Denmark Street.
➕ G5 ✉ 24 Litchfield Street, WC2 ☎ 020 7240 4158 🚇 Leicester Square

CHINA & GLASS

ARAM DESIGNS LTD
Aram's international modern design includes works by Depadova.
➕ G5 ✉ 3 Kean Street, WC2 ☎ 020 7240 3933 🚇 Aldwych or Covent Garden

ARIA
Aria stocks modern international state-of-the-art design, with plenty of Italian pieces on display. There is a second shop across the road devoted to bathroom accessories.
➕ H2 ✉ 133 Upper Street, N1 ☎ 020 7226 1021 🚇 Angel

CERAMICA BLUE
Huge collection of functional and decorative contemporary ceramic designs, made exclusively by potters from all over the world.
➕ A5 ✉ 10 Blenheim Crescent, W11 ☎ 020 7727 0288 🚇 Ladbroke Grove

DESIGNER'S GUILD
Tricia Guild's store is a wonderland of exquisite design. Contemporary china, glass, and irresistible fabrics.
➕ D8 ✉ 277 King's Road, SW3 ☎ 020 7351 5775 🚇 Sloane Square then 15 minutes' walk or bus 19 or 22

HABITAT
Founded by Sir Terence Conran (▶ 9), this modern furniture store also stocks glass, china, and household goods.
➕ F4 ✉ 196 Tottenham Court Road, W1 ☎ 020 7631 3880 🚇 Goodge Street

HEAL'S
A frontrunner of the Arts and Crafts movement in the 1920s, Heal's specializes in timeless contemporary furniture.
➕ F4 ✉ 196 Tottenham Court Road, W1 ☎ 020 7636 1666 🚇 Goodge Street

INFINITY
Some of the best modern glassware in town, specializing in wine glasses, goblets, fruit bowls, and vases; colors are jewel-like.
➕ G5 ✉ 8 Upper St Martin's Lane, WC2 ☎ 020 7497 1011 🚇 Leicester Square

JEANETTE HAYHURST
One of the few places to find old glass, especially British pieces. Also stocks interesting studio glass.
➕ B6 ✉ 32a Kensington Church Street, W8 ☎ 020 7938 1539 🚇 High Street Kensington

THOMAS GOODE & CO
Collectors of Meissen and Dresden need look no further than this splendid showroom. Also stockists of Lalique and Baccarat crystal.
➕ E6 ✉ 19 South Audley Street, W1 ☎ 020 7499 2823 🚇 Green Park

WATERFORD WEDGWOOD
The largest selection of handmade, full lead crystal Waterford glass—all made in Ireland—and Wedgwood china. Will phone the factory for special orders, help customers search for designs no longer made, and ship goods worldwide.
➕ F5 ✉ 173–4 Piccadilly, W1 ☎ 020 7629 2614 🚇 Piccadilly Circus

> Do not worry about breaking your valuable purchases on the way home; they can be packed and sent there for you, fully insured.

Silver

English silver is one of the best antiques buys because it has been hallmarked since the mid-17th century, so you know precisely what you are buying. To get a good look, wander the London Silver Vaults on Chancery Lane, Antiquarius (▶ 73), Gray's Antique Market (▶ 73), Asprey's on Bond Street, Garrard and Mappin & Webb on Regent Street (▶ 70). Buy at these locations or visit Christine Schell (✉ 15 Cale Street, SW3) for silver and tortoiseshell, or John Jesse (✉ 160 Kensington Church Street, W8) for art deco.

MUSEUM & GALLERY SHOPS

Specialty shops

Specialty shops come in every shape and size. Stanley Gibbons (✉ 399 Strand, WC2) is a philatelist's paradise, while James Smith & Sons (✉ 53 New Oxford Street, W1) stocks every kind of umbrella to keep British rain at bay. Other favorites include Christopher Farr (✉ 115 Regent's Park Road, NW1) for contemporary carpets, the Crafts Council Shop (✉ 44 Pentonville Road, N1 and at the V&A ➤ 28), Creativity (✉ 45 New Oxford Street, WC1) for needlework materials, Paperchase (✉ 213 Tottenham Court Road, W1) and Smythson's (✉ 44 New Bond Street, W1), both stationers. To find the specialty shop you want, use the Yellow Pages telephone directory, which is listed by subject.

BRITISH LIBRARY
(➤ 54)
Plenty of books, but other collection-inspired objects, too.

BRITISH MUSEUM
(➤ 43)
Books, games, and design objects. Especially strong on Egypt influence goods.

DESIGN MUSEUM
(➤ 50)
Extensive and immensely chic designer goods, some with high price tags.

LONDON AQUARIUM
(➤ 51)
The world beneath the seas packaged to delight and educate.

MUSEUM OF LONDON
(➤ 47)
Good for souvenirs and books about London.

NATIONAL GALLERY
(➤ 39)
Two large shops; particularly good for paper goods and diaries.

NATIONAL PORTRAIT GALLERY (➤ 38)
Surprisingly large store, well stocked with books on historical figures and British history; own-brand children's book projects.

NATURAL HISTORY MUSEUM (➤ 26)
Thousands of dinosaurs to read about, cut out or put on the mantelpiece; plus plenty about the world since then.

POLLOCK TOY MUSEUM (➤ 51)
Cramped, but like an Aladdin's cave for children. Toys of all prices including Pollock's toy theaters.

QUEEN'S GALLERY & ROYAL MEWS (➤ 32)
The largest selection of publications and memorabilia about the British royal family.

ROYAL ACADEMY
(➤ 51)
If you cannot own a work by a Royal Academician, then buy a plate, mug, pen, or book specially designed by one for the RA store.

ROYAL BOTANICAL GARDENS, KEW
(➤ 24)
Comprehensive selection of goods and publications—many lavishly illustrated to keep the most ardent gardener happy.

SCIENCE MUSEUM
(➤ 27)
Plenty of books and projects for budding scientists of all ages.

TATE GALLERIES
(➤ 34)
The annual Tate diary, its pages scattered with reproductions from the Modern and British collections, is a collector's item; also an extensive collection of quality posters.

VICTORIA & ALBERT MUSEUM (➤ 28)
You could do a full-scale Christmas shop here, from toys and books to unique crafts. Many collection-inspired goods.

FOOD & WINE

BERRY BROS & RUDD
Opened as a grocery store in 1699; the wines range from popular varieties to specialty madeiras, ports, and clarets. Their own-label bottles are also good value. Perfect service.
✚ F6 ✉ 3 St. James's Street, SW1 ☎ 020 7396 9600 Ⓜ Green Park

THE BLOOMSBURY WINE AND SPIRIT COMPANY
In addition to wines, the strength of this store is its Scottish malt whiskeys: more than 170 in stock.
✚ G4 ✉ 3 Bloomsbury Street, WC1 ☎ 020 7436 4763/4 Ⓜ Tottenham Court Road

CARLUCCIO'S
A designer deli stocking only the most refined goods, such as truffle oil, black pasta, and balsamic vinegar.
✚ G5 ✉ 30 Neal Street, WC2 ☎ 020 7240 1487 Ⓜ Covent Garden

DRONES, THE GROCER
Deli attached to a restaurant. Fresh bread, cold meats, cheese, sauces, and luxury packaged goods that make great presents.
✚ E7 ✉ 3 Pont Street, SW1 ☎ 020 7259 6188 Ⓜ Knightsbridge

FRATELLI CAMISA
One of London's best-loved Italian delis.
✚ F5 ✉ 53 Charlotte Street, W1 ☎ 020 7255 1240 Ⓜ Goodge Street

NEAL'S YARD DAIRY
A temple to the British cheese, where more than 50 varieties from small farms in Britain are ripened to perfection.
✚ G5 ✉ 17 Shorts Gardens, WC2 ☎ 020 7379 7646 Ⓜ Covent Garden

ODDBINS
With more than 60 branches in London, Oddbins is strong on quality, range, and price.
✚ G5 ✉ 23 Earlham Street, WC2 ☎ 020 7836 6331 Ⓜ Covent Garden

ROCOCO
Delicious, imaginative chocolates—go for artisan bars flavored with Earl Grey tea, chili pepper, nutmeg, cardamom, or wild mint leaves.
✚ D8 ✉ 321 King's Road, SW3 ☎ 020 7352 5857 Ⓜ Sloane Square

TOM'S
Basement deli sells breads, patisserie, cheeses, cold meats, preserved lemons, olives, and caviar. Bustling café on the first floor.
✚ B5 ✉ 226 Westbourne Grove, W11 ☎ 020 7221 8818 Ⓜ Bayswater

VILLANDRY
Quality "foodstore" with best buys taking in French and English cheeses, great breads, olive oil, and much more.
✚ F5 ✉ 170 Great Portland Street W1N ☎ 020 7631 3131 Ⓜ Great Portland Street

WILD OATS
Five hundred customers a day explore the three floors of quality whole and organic food.
✚ B5 ✉ 210 Westbourne Grove, W11 ☎ 020 7229 1063 Ⓜ Notting Hill Gate or Westbourne Park

Wine

London has an unrivaled variety of international wines at the best prices, for, although Britain is not a major wine-producing country, the British like to drink wine and know about it. This explains the range, quality, and fiercely competitive prices in the chains (Oddbins, Threshers) and the supermarkets (Sainsbury's, Safeway, Waitrose, and Tesco). For bulk buying, consider the Majestic Warehouse chain, a reliable wine merchant, or Christie's and Sotheby's regular wine auctions (➤ 73).

Make a picnic

With so many parks and benches to choose from in London, a picnic makes a good break from a hard morning's sightseeing or shopping. The big stores have some of the most seductive food halls—and they stock wine; see Harrods, Selfridges, Fortnum & Mason, and Marks & Spencer (all ➤ 71). Old Compton Street (➤ 70) is a food shopper's delight; see also And Clarke's Bakery (✉ 122 Kensington Church Street, W8) and other cafés that sell their own prepared food to take away.

THEATER

Theater tips

If you care about where you sit, go in person and peruse the plan. For an evening "Sold out" performance, it is worth lining up for returns; otherwise, try for a matinée. The most inexpensive seats could be far from the stage or uncomfortable, so take binoculars and a cushion. As for dress, Londoners rarely dress up for the theater anymore; but they do order their intermission drinks before the play starts, and remain seated while they applaud.

Ticket–buying tips

Use the SOLT Half-price Ticket Booth. Preview tickets are lower in price, as are matinée tickets. Get up early and line up for one-day bargain tickets at the RNT. Go with friends and make a party booking at a reduced rate. Ask the National Theatre, RSC, Royal Court, and other theaters about special discounts on particular performances; and keep student and senior citizen cards ready. Remember, the show is the same wherever you sit!

Theater in London covers a wide range of venues. It is vibrant, varied, and extensive. The following is intended to help theatergoers find the experience they want.

INFORMATION

Time Out, London's weekly entertainment guide, provides an exhaustive list of all theaters, plus reviews. Daily newspapers carry a less complete but totally up-to-date listing, with more reviews. Ticket prices are lowest for fringe, more expensive for West End and very expensive for musicals.

TICKET BUYING

Telephone booking can be done with a credit card, which must be produced when collecting the tickets. If you book without a credit card, you must usually arrive at the theater 40 minutes before curtain-up—or else the tickets will be put back for sale. Booking in person means you can see the seating plan—a good idea if you want a decent seat in some of London's older theaters. Ask for information on leg room and sight lines.

TICKET AGENCIES

Ticketmaster ☎ 020 7344 4444 and First Call ☎ 020 7420 0000 are both reliable. Some shows have no booking fee, others a small one, and a few rise to 22 percent of ticket price, so ask first. Beware: it is unwise to buy from small agencies, and very unwise to buy from scalpers.

SOLT HALF-PRICE TICKET BOOTH

Each day a limited number of tickets for some West End shows is sold for that day's performance at half price, plus a £2 service charge. The rules are: no credit cards; a maximum of four tickets per person, no exchanges or returns.
✚ G5 ✉ Leicester Square, WC2 🕐 Mon–Sat 1–6:30; matinée days noon–6:30 🚇 Leicester Square or Piccadilly Circus

THE THEATER YEAR

The theaters are never dark. At any one time there will be an average of 45 West End theaters playing a range of musicals, drama, comedy, and thrillers, as well as staging opera and dance. For festivals, many with theatrical events (► 22). LIFT (the London International Festival of Theatre) takes place in July and August in alternate years. The Royal Shakespeare Company (RSC) holds an annual festival, often at the Almeida theater.

WEST END THEATERS

The Society of London Theatres (SOLT) represents the owners, managers, and producers of 54 major London theaters. SOLT runs the annual Lawrence Olivier Awards—London's answer to the Tonys—publishes the fortnightly London Theatre Guide (free from theaters), and runs a Theatre Token scheme ☎ 020 7240 8800 and the SOLT Half-price Ticket Booth (see above).

ROYAL NATIONAL THEATRE (RNT)

British and world drama, classics and new plays. Home of the National Theatre company, it has three performance spaces—the Olivier, the Lyttelton, and the Cottesloe. All have several productions in repertory.

🚇 H6 ✉ South Bank, SE1 ☎ Information and tours 020 7452 3400. Theater tickets 020 7452 3000 🚇 Embankment or Waterloo 🚆 Waterloo

ROYAL SHAKESPEARE THEATRE (RSC)

The London home of the Royal Shakespeare Company, who perform in season in the Barbican Theatre (level 3) and The Pit (level 1). Some productions are new, others are from Stratford; several productions may be running concurrently in repertory. There is an annual Prom season, plus backstage tours.

🚇 J4 ✉ Barbican Centre, Silk Street, EC2 ☎ 020 7638 4141. Reservations (and recorded information after 8PM) 020 7638 8891. Range of good ticket deals 🚇 Barbican

MUSICALS

The successful, long-running shows are dominated by the great impresarios. Sir Andrew Lloyd Webber, who restored and owns the Palace Theatre, has staged *Starlight Express*, *Sunset Boulevard*, *Phantom of the Opera*, and *Cats*, the latter two with Cameron Mackintosh, who has had great success with his *Les Misérables*.

LONG-RUNNING STALWARTS

Few plays have the sustained, long-running success of the musicals. Most famous is Agatha Christie's *The Mousetrap* at St. Martin's, aiming for its 50th anniversary in 2002. At the Fortune Theatre, *The Woman in Black* began its run in 1989.

OFF–WEST END THEATER

This new category honors the fringe theaters that still stage imaginative productions. Look in the listings for the Almeida, the Bush, Donmar Warehouse, Drill Hall, the Gate, Hampstead, ICA, King's Head, Lyric Studio, Riverside Studios, Royal Court, Theatre Royal Stratford East, Tricycle, the Young Vic.

FRINGE AND PUB THEATER

True fringe, or "alternative" theater in London is vibrant, varied, and dotted about in over 35 venues, many of them pubs. Try Etcetera Theatre (at the Oxford Arms pub), Finborough, the Hen & Chickens, Man in the Moon, New End Theatre, Old Red Lion, and the White Bear.

COMEDY

The Comedy Store is hugely popular. Also try the Hurricane Club, Banana Cabaret, Jongleurs at the Cornet, Comedy Café, Red Rose Cabaret, and Hackney Empire, a restored music hall that holds vaudeville nights.

Open-air theater

If the weather is good, grab a picnic and head for the Open Air Theatre, Regent's Park (Jun–Sep), Greenwich Old Observatory (Jul–Aug), or Holland Park Theatre (Jun–Aug).

Children's theater

Several theaters stage magical performances all year around. Names to look for include the Little Angel Marionette Theatre (doyen of puppet theaters), Polka Children's Theatre, and the Unicorn Theatre for Children. Ask about children's productions at the National and the RSC, as well as Punch and Judy shows in Covent Garden Piazza.

Revived theaters

Some old London theaters have been revived. Andrew Lloyd Webber restored his 1880s Cambridge Theatre. The Theatre Royal, Haymarket, has new gold leaf, while the Savoy and the Criterion have been meticulously restored. Out of the West End, the Richmond Theatre and Islington's Collins Music Hall have reopened. On the south bank, Sir Peter Hall's company is in the revived Old Vic Theatre and a small-scale Globe theater opened in 1997, designed in the manner of Burbage's original where Shakespeare worked.

CLASSICAL MUSIC, OPERA & BALLET

Food with music

The choice is wide (➤ 81). For starters, there are tea dances at Le Meridien Waldorf (➤ 67). Claridges' cocktails with their Hungarian Quartet are an institution, while a dinner dance at the Savoy, Ritz, and Claridges is opulently romantic (➤ 84). Rock Garden (✉ 5–6 The Piazza, Covent Garden, WC2), Deals West (✉ 14–16 Foubert's Place, W1), Break for the Border (✉ 8 Argyll Street, W1), and Pizza Pomodoro (✉ 51 Beauchamp Place, SW3) are altogether more informal. But if the weather is good, do as Londoners do and head for a park (see panel Music everywhere! opposite).

Glyndebourne

Glyndebourne Festival Opera (late May–Aug) is only a train ride away in Sussex (✉ Glyndebourne, Lewes, Sussex BN8 5UU ☎ 01273 813813). Performances begin late afternoon, with long intervals for picnics in the sumptuous grounds. It makes a delightful outing, and the train service is good.

THE MUSIC YEAR

Runs non stop. Look for festivals such as the City of London, Spitalfields, Almeida and Hampton Court Palace, and traditions such as the Christmas Oratorios, carol singing in Trafalgar Square, and the Easter Passions. The major classic festival is the Proms, a nickname for the Henry Wood Promenade Concerts, held daily at the Royal Albert Hall and elsewhere from mid-July to mid-September, and broadcast live on BBC Radio 3.

THE DANCE YEAR

Very lively, with great variety. Highpoints include the Coliseum's summer season, the Royal Ballet's performances at the Royal Opera House, and the Nutcracker Suite season at the Royal Festival Hall (Dec–Jan). Other major venues are: Sadler's Wells, the Place, ICA, and Riverside Studios. The climax of the year is Dance Umbrella, a world showcase for contemporary dance (Oct–Nov).

THE OPERA YEAR

Grand opera alternates with dance at the Royal Opera House. Cheaper and often more vibrant opera takes place at the larger Coliseum (performances in English). In addition, there are visits from Welsh National Opera, Opera North and Opera Factory, and open-air opera performances in Holland Park and by Kenwood Lake.

MAJOR VENUES

BARBICAN CONCERT HALL
✚ J4 ✉ Barbican Centre, Silk Street, EC2 ☎ 020 7638 4141. Reservations (and recorded information after 8PM) 020 7638 8891. Credit card reservations 020 7638 8891, daily 9–8. Range of good ticket deals
🚇 Barbican

LONDON COLISEUM
✚ G5 ✉ St. Martin's Lane, WC2 ☎ 020 7632 8300
🚇 Leicester Square

ROYAL ALBERT HALL
✚ C6 ✉ Kensington Gore, SW7 ☎ 020 7589 3203. Reservations 020 7589 8212
🚇 South Kensington

ROYAL OPERA HOUSE
Undergoing alterations. Alternative venues.
✚ G5 ✉ Covent Garden, WC2 ☎ 020 7304 4000 🚇 Covent Garden

SADLER'S WELLS THEATRE
The most electrifying dance theater in Europe—a must for all ballet fans.
✚ H3 ✉ Rosebery Avenue, EC1 ☎ 020 7312 1996
🚇 Angel

SOUTH BANK
Royal Festival Hall, Queen Elizabeth Hall, and Purcell Room.
✚ G6–H6 ✉ South Bank, SE1 ☎ 020 7921 0600
🚇 Waterloo

WIGMORE HALL
✚ E5 ✉ 36 Wigmore Street, W1 ☎ 020 7935 2141
🚇 Bond Street

JAZZ & PUB MUSIC

London boasts a great concentration of world-class jazz musicians, both homegrown and foreign, traditional and contemporary—look out for Camden Jazz Week, Capital Jazz Festival, and the Bracknell Festival. Evening and late-night gigs cover rock, roots, rhythm and blues, and more, many in pubs. For a list of venues, check *Time Out*.

THE AVENUE
A sleek minimalist setting for an upbeat Sunday brunch, served to the cool sounds of a jazz singer with pianist backing.
➕ F5 ☒ 7–9 St James's Street, SW1 ☎ 020 7321 2111 🔘 Green Park

BRICKLAYERS ARMS
Popular pub in upcoming Shoreditch crammed with students and artists. DJs play the newest sounds weekends.
➕ J4 ☒ 63 Charlotte Road, EC2 ☎ 020 7739 5245 🔘 Old Street

BULL'S HEAD, BARNES
Seductive combination of good jazz in the friendly village atmosphere of a riverside pub.
➕ Off map at A10 ☒ 373 Lonsdale Road, SW13 ☎ 020 8876 5241

DOVER STREET
Large, candle-lit, popular basement where the music can be jump jive, jazz, rhythm and blues, or Big Band. The food is good.
➕ F6 ☒ 8–9 Dover Street, W1 ☎ 020 7629 9813 🔘 Piccadilly Circus

HALF MOON PUTNEY
Jolly pub for rhythm and blues played by lesser stars; plenty of audience participation.
➕ Off map at A10 ☒ 93 Lower Richmond Road, SW15 ☎ 020 8780 9383

JAZZ CAFÉ
Current favorite among the young; buzzes nightly with the widest range of jazz, from soul to rap.
➕ F2 ☒ 5 Parkway, NW1 ☎ 020 7916 6060 🔘 Camden Town

PIZZA EXPRESS, SOHO
Quality pizzas and great, often mainstream, jazz in this friendly Soho cellar. Several other branches of Pizza Express have live jazz, too.
➕ F5 ☒ 10 Dean Street, W1 ☎ 020 7439 8722 🔘 Tottenham Court Road

PIZZA ON THE PARK
More upscale than its sister, Pizza Express; top foreign names play at one or other venue.
➕ E6 ☒ 11 Knightsbridge, SW1 ☎ 020 7235 5273 🔘 Hyde Park Corner

RONNIE SCOTT'S
One of the world's best-known and most loved jazz clubs, run by jazz musicians for jazz lovers.
➕ F5 ☒ 47 Frith Street, W1 ☎ 020 7439 0747 🔘 Tottenham Court Road

WHITE HORSE
Huge, lively tavern with front terrace that's packed in summer. Popular jazz duo Sunday evenings.
➕ B9 ☒ 1 Parsons Green, SW6 ☎ 020 7736 2115 🔘 Parsons Green

Pub music

This can be one of the least expensive and most enjoyable evenings out in London, worth the trip to an off-beat location. For the price of a pint of beer (usually a huge choice) you can settle down to enjoy the ambience and listen to some of the best alternative music available in town—from folk, jazz and blues to rhythm and blues, soul, and more. Audiences tend to be friendly, loyal to their venue, and happy to talk music.

Music everywhere!

London is full of music. At lunchtime, the best places are churches, where the regular concerts are usually free. Look in *Time Out* listings (➤ 79) for: St. Anne, St. Agnes, and St. Olave's in the City; St. James's, Piccadilly, in the West End. St. Paul's Cathedral evensong is mid-afternoon. On Sundays, cathedrals and churches are again best for sacred music. Look for concerts in historic houses, museums and galleries, especially during the City of London Festival (July). Finally, music is played outdoors in the royal parks, Embankment Gardens, and elsewhere, but best of all at Kenwood (➤ 29) or Marble Hill, Richmond, on summer evenings.

81

MOVIES & CLUBS

London lacks the range of movie theaters to be found in some other cities and often receives foreign films long after their home release. But there is plenty of independent and late-night cinema, making a good beginning to a night of clubbing. Some cinema seats are half price on Mondays.

One-night clubbing is strong. To find the right club night and club style, consult *Time Out*'s night-by-night listing (➤ 78) or see the advertisements at regular venues. Dress streetwise and pay at the door.

Cocktails and bars

Apart from a handful, including Mezzo (✉ 100 Wardour Street, W1), the best bars are in hotels. For plushness, the Lanesborough (✉ Hyde Park Corner, SW1) and Langham (✉ Langham Place, SW1) are best. For pampering, head for the Savoy's Thames Foyer and Claridge's lounge (➤ 84). For New York style try the Savoy's American Bar (➤ 84). To be seen, go to the Dorchester (✉ Park Lane, W1). To be discreet, go to the Connaught (✉ 16 Carlos Place, W1). London's best private bar is at Morton's, a club in Berkeley Square that offers temporary membership.

CINEMAS

THE BIG SCREENS
The places to see premiers and commercial first runs. Biggest are the Empire (Cinema 1) and Odeon on Leicester Square, the ABC on Shaftesbury Avenue, and the Odeon Marble Arch.

IMAX CINEMAS (➤ 58)
For a truly spectacular wraparound cinematic experince.

THE INDEPENDENTS
Show mainstream blockbusters, foreign (subtitled), and offbeat British movies. The most sumptuous are Minema, Lumière, Curzon Mayfair, Barbican, and the Chelsea Cinema; others include the Screen chain, Camden Plaza, Gate, Metro, and Renoir.

NATIONAL FILM THEATRE
Advantages of its two screens: good programing, silent audiences, movie-specialist bookstore, riverside restaurant, children's screenings.
🚇 H6 ✉ South Bank, SE1 ☎ 020 7928 3232 🚇 Waterloo

REPERTORY
Good for old movies, seasons, double-bills, and late nights. Try the Everyman and the Phoenix; knife-edge contemporary at ICA Cinemathèque; variety at the French and Goethe Institutes. Also go to the Museum of London's "Made in London" series (➤ 47).

CLUB VENUES

BORDERLINE
Mill with music business insiders at this lively basement.
🚇 G5 ✉ Orange Yard, off Manette Street, W1 ☎ 020 7734 2095 🚇 Tottenham Court Road

CAMDEN PALACE
Friendly ambience for a bargain night out. Indie bands on Tuesdays.
🚇 F2 ✉ 1a Camden High Street, NW1 ☎ 020 7387 0428 🚇 Mornington Crescent

THE EQUINOX
The best for an energetic bop on a crowded floor.
🚇 G5 ✉ Leicester Square, WC2 ☎ 020 7437 1446 🚇 Leicester Square

THE GARDENING CLUB
Covent Garden's busiest.
🚇 G5 ✉ 4 The Piazza, WC2 ☎ 020 7497 3154 🚇 Covent Garden

MINISTRY OF SOUND
London's hottest club is the most reliable of new wave. House and jazz Saturdays.
🚇 J7 ✉ 103 Gaunt Street, SE1 ☎ 020 7378 6528 🚇 Elephant & Castle

THE VENUE
Worth the journey to hear the best indie bands.
🚇 N9 ✉ 2a Clifton Rise, New Cross, SE14 ☎ 020 8692 4077 🚇 New Cross or New Cross Gate.

SOUND REPUBLIC
Soho spot for modern soul, rhythm and blues, and hip-hop jams.
🚇 F5 ✉ 10 Wardour Street, W1 ☎ 020 7287 1010 🚇 Leicester Square

SPECTATOR SPORTS

You can watch and play most sports either in or near London (often merely an underground ride away). Major events are held on Saturdays and Sundays; tickets are readily available (see ticket agencies ➤ 78–79).

THE MAJOR VENUES

ALL ENGLAND LAWN TENNIS CHAMPIONSHIPS, WIMBLEDON

Tennis's top tournament starts late June. Enter the ticket ballot or join lines for tickets, except on the last four days.

✉ All England Lawn Tennis and Croquet Club, Church Road, SW19 ☎ 020 8946 2244 Ⓢ Southfields

CRYSTAL PALACE NATIONAL SPORTS CENTRE

The major venue for national competitions.

✉ Ledrington Road SE19 ☎ 020 8778 0131 🚉 Crystal Palace

LORD'S CRICKET GROUND

Home of the MCC (Marylebone Cricket Club ➤ 60); watch Middlesex play home games, test cricket, major finals, and Sunday league games.

➕ D3 ✉ St. John's Wood Road, NW8 ☎ 020 7432 1066 Ⓢ St. John's Wood

THE OVAL

Surrey home games and test cricket; also Sunday league games.

➕ H8 ✉ Surrey County Cricket Club, The Oval, SE11 ☎ 020 7582 6660 Ⓢ Oval

ROYAL ALBERT HALL

Grand Victorian building holding 5,000 spectators; boxing, tennis, and sumo-wrestling events.

➕ C6 ✉ Kensington Gore, SW7 ☎ 020 7589 8212 Ⓢ South Kensington

WEMBLEY STADIUM AND ARENA

A vast complex with Stadium, Arena and Conference and Exhibition Centre. Stadium currently undergoing rebuilding.

✉ Wembley, Middlesex ☎ 020 8900 1234. Tours 020 8902 8833 Ⓢ Wembley Park

OTHER MAJOR SPORTS

ASSOCIATION FOOTBALL (SOCCER)

To see the FA Cup final (May) at Wembley, pay high prices; alternatively, visit one of the 12 London clubs (Aug–May) such as Arsenal, Chelsea, Fulham, or Tottenham Hotspur.

AUTO RACING

Plenty of action at Brands Hatch in Kent: racing most weekends of the year, usually motorcycles on Saturdays, cars on Sundays.

RUGBY UNION

Tickets for the internationals at Twickenham are scarce; it is easier to watch the Varsity match (Dec), the Cup Final (Apr–May) or take in a tour game, and easier still to watch a game at one of the ten London clubs such as Blackheath or Harlequins.

Participatory sports

London's many parks and open spaces are alive with people playing tennis, bowls, cricket and soccer, or jogging, walking, and boating. For more formal sports, Crystal Palace National Sports Centre has comprehensive facilities; but Kensington Sports Centre (✉ Walmer Road, W1), the Oasis (✉ 32 Endell Street, WC2), and the Queen Mother Sports Centre (✉ 223 Vauxhall Bridge Road, SW1) are more central. Barbican Health & Fitness Centre and Broadgate Club (at the Broadgate Centre, ➤ 54) have good fitness equipment.

Horse racing

A British obsession, so there are plenty of races near London during the flat season (Mar–Nov) and winter steeplechasing (Aug–May). On and off course, betting is legal and well governed. Daytime races at Newmarket, Epsom, Goodwood, and Ascot can be reached by train from London, or take the train out to Windsor or Kempton for a delightful summer evening meeting. Daily newspapers have details of race meetings.

83

LUXURY HOTELS

Prices

Expect to pay the following prices per night for a single room:

Luxury   more than £210

Mid-range   up to £130

Budget   up to £70

Bargain deals

To be pampered amid sumptuous surroundings may be an essential part of your vacation. London's most luxurious hotels have been built with no expense spared. Although London hotel prices are generally very high, quality rooms can be had for bargain prices. It's always worth asking when you make your reservation whether any special deals are available. Most deluxe and mid-range hotels offer weekend deals throughout the year, often including breakfast, dinner, and sometimes theater tickets. The big chains such as Forte, Mount Charlotte Thistle, and Best Western have brochures offering package deals. Newly refurbished hotels usually have incentive prices, and off-season months such as January and February are a buyer's market.

CLARIDGE'S
From the art deco lobby and mirrored dining room to the huge baths and log fires in the corner suites, this is deluxe Mayfair living.
➕ E5 ✉ Brook Street, W1
☎ 020 7629 8860, fax 020 7499 2210 🚇 Bond Street

FOUR SEASONS HOTEL
Formerly called Inn on the Park, this modern hotel may lack period style, but it provides some of the best service in town.
➕ E6 ✉ Hamilton Place, Park Lane, W1 ☎ 020 7499 0888, fax 020 7493 6629 🚇 Hyde Park Corner

GORING
High standards of old-fashioned hospitality and service make this splendid hotel memorable. Owned by the Goring family for almost a century.
➕ F7 ✉ Beeston Place, Grosvenor Gardens, SW1
☎ 020 7396 9000, fax 020 7834 4393 🚇 Victoria

HALKIN HOTEL
Central London's first deluxe hotel built and furnished in contemporary design throughout, with a suitably upscale Italian restaurant. Ideal location for visits to Knightsbridge and Mayfair.
➕ E6 ✉ 4 Halkin Street, SW1
☎ 020 7333 1000, fax 020 7333 1100 🚇 Hyde Park Corner

MANDARIN ORIENTAL HYDE PARK
New owners are injecting new life back into this grand hotel. Top-class service. Stunning views over Hyde Park.
➕ E6 ✉ Knightsbridge, SW1
☎ 020 7235 2000, fax 020 7235 4552 🚇 Knightsbridge

LE MERIDIEN PICCADILLY
Residents can use Champneys health club, which fills the basement; French influence in the well-appointed rooms.
➕ F6 ✉ 21 Piccadilly, W1
☎ 020 7734 8000, fax 020 7437 3574 🚇 Piccadilly Circus

THE RITZ
Small but sumptuous, with plenty of old style, gilt decor and the great first-floor promenade to London's most beautiful dining room, overlooking Green Park.
➕ F6 ✉ Piccadilly W1
☎ 020 7493 8181, fax 020 7493 2687 🚇 Green Park

SAVOY
Old-style Thameside hotel between the West End and the City; splendid river suites; art deco rooms; health club.
➕ G5 ✉ Strand, WC2
☎ 020 7836 4343, fax 020 7872 8901 🚇 Aldwych or Embankment

THE STAFFORD
Tucked behind Piccadilly, with an alley through to Green Park, this is a small, discreet hotel whose cozy, intimate public rooms are open to non-guests.
➕ F6 ✉ 16 St. James's Place, SW1 ☎ 020 7493 0111, fax 020 7493 7121 🚇 Green Park

MID-RANGE HOTELS

ACADEMY

Excellent location for the British Museum; a delightful combination of four converted Georgian town houses with exceptionally light, modern rooms.

➕ F4 ✉ 17–21 Gower Street, WC1 ☎ 020 7631 4115, fax 020 7636 3442 Ⓖ Goodge Street

BASIL STREET HOTEL

Tucked behind Harrods and full of old-style comforts, favored by discerning Americans.

➕ D7 ✉ Basil Street, SW3 ☎ 020 7581 3311, fax 020 7581 3693 Ⓖ Knightsbridge

5 SUMNER PLACE HOTEL

Family-run house-hotel, in a chic South Kensington residential area; a dozen rooms, and a garden.

➕ C7 ✉ 5 Sumner Place, SW7 ☎ 020 7584 7586, fax 020 7823 9962 Ⓖ South Kensington

HOTEL NUMBER SIXTEEN

Long-established champion of the many delightful London house-hotels (converted from four Victorian houses); log fires, walled garden.

➕ C7 ✉ 16 Sumner Place, SW7 ☎ 020 7589 5232, fax 020 7584 8615 Ⓖ South Kensington

THE LEONARD

Discreet, stylish small hotel, two minutes' walk from Oxford Street; comfortable, superbly decorated bedrooms.

➕ D5 ✉ 15 Seymour Street, W1 ☎ 020 7935 2010, fax 020 7935 6700 Ⓖ Marble Arch

LONDON MARRIOTT COUNTY HALL

The former Greater London Council building makes the most of its river views—Big Ben, Houses of Parliament—plus an excellent range of leisure facilities to accompany the well-laid out bedrooms.

➕ G6 ✉ County Hall, SE1 ☎ 020 7928 5200, fax 020 7928 5300 Ⓖ Westminster

MANDEVILLE

Busy, international hotel with multilingual reception staff yet a peaceful location in the heart of the West End.

➕ E5 ✉ Mandeville Place, W1 ☎ 020 7935 5599, fax 020 7935 9588 Ⓖ Bond Street

THE MONTAGUE ON THE GARDENS

Bloomsbury houses converted into a traditional hotel; terrace and garden.

➕ G4 ✉ 15 Montague Street, WC1 ☎ 020 7637 1001, fax 020 7637 2516 Ⓖ Holborn or Russell Square

REMBRANDT

Large Edwardian hotel ideal for Knightsbridge and South Kensington, with a health club.

➕ D7 ✉ 11 Thurloe Place, SW7 ☎ 020 7589 8100, fax 020 7225 3363 Ⓖ South Kensington

THE RUBENS AT THE PALACE

Comfortable hotel opposite the Royal Mews behind Buckingham Palace.

➕ F7 ✉ Buckingham Palace Road, SW1 ☎ 020 7834 6600, fax 020 7233 6037 Ⓖ Victoria

Beware of hidden hotel costs

The room price quoted by a hotel may, or may not, include continental breakfast or full English breakfast and VAT, which is currently 17½ percent. Since these affect the final bill dramatically, it is vital to check. Also, check the percentage mark-up on telephone calls, which can be high—there may even be charges for using a telephone charge card or receiving a fax; and ask about the laundry and pressing service, which can be very slow.

85

BUDGET ACCOMMODATIONS

Location is everything

It is well worth perusing the London map to decide where you are likely to spend most of your time. Then select a hotel in that area or accessible to it by underground on a direct line, so you avoid having to change trains. London is vast and it takes time to cross it, particularly by bus and costly taxis. By paying a little more to be in the center and near your activities, you will save on travel time and costs.

Youth hostels

There are seven hostels in central London (by Oxford Street, in Holland Park, and by St. Paul's Cathedral, for example), so reserve well ahead.

Youth Hostels Association
✉ Trevelyan House, 8 St. Stephen's Hill, St. Albans, Hertfordshire AL1 2DY ☎ 01727 855215, fax 01727 844126. Reservations 020 7373 3400, fax 020 7236 7681

EURO HOTEL
Stylish Bloomsbury setting for a small, charming bed and breakfast.
✚ G4 ✉ 51–3 Cartwright Gardens, Russell Square, WC1 ☎ 020 7387 4321, fax 020 7383 5044 🚇 Russell Square

HENLEY HOUSE HOTEL
Attractive Victorian house in a tidy garden square.
✚ B7 ✉ 30 Barkston Gardens, SW5 ☎ 020 7370 4111, fax 020 7370 0026 🚇 Earl's Court

INTERNATIONAL STUDENTS HOUSE
Rooms and family flats right by Regent's Park. Reserve well ahead.
✚ F4 ✉ 229 Great Portland Street, W1 ☎ 020 7631 8300, fax 020 7631 8315 🚇 Great Portland Street or Regent's Park

KENSINGTON MANOR HOTEL
Modest small hotel, ideally placed for South Kensington museums and Knightsbridge shopping.
✚ C7 ✉ 8 Emperors Gate, SW7 ☎ 020 7370 7516, fax 020 7373 3163 🚇 Gloucester Road

LONDON HOMESTEAD SERVICES
Try this agency if you want to stay with a London family: 200 homes within 20 minutes of Piccadilly. Minimum 3-night stay.
✉ Coombe Wood Road, Kingston-upon-Thames, Surrey ☎ 020 8949 4455, fax 020 8549 5492

MELBOURNE HOUSE HOTEL
Family-run, private hotel within walking distance of Victoria station.
✚ F7 ✉ 79 Belgrave Road, SW1 ☎ 020 7828 3516, fax 020 7828 7120 🚇 Victoria

MENTONE HOTEL
Simple, relaxing rooms in a pleasant bed and breakfast.
✚ G4 ✉ 54–6 Cartwright Gardens, Russell Square, WC1 ☎ 020 7387 3927, fax 020 7388 4671 🚇 Russell Square

SWISS HOUSE HOTEL
Comfortable little hotel in a pretty residential area of South Kensington.
✚ C8 ✉ 171 Old Brompton Road, SW5 ☎ 020 7373 2769, fax 020 7373 4983 🚇 Earl's Court or Gloucester Road

UNIVERSITY WOMEN'S CLUB
Two dozen rooms in an old Mayfair house; membership open to all women graduates and similarly qualified women; friends pay a temporary membership fee.
✚ E6 ✉ 2 Audley Square, South Audley Street, W1 ☎ 020 7499 2268, fax 020 7499 7046 🚇 Hyde Park Corner

VICTORIA INN
Friendly, stucco-fronted Pimlico house with practical, no-frills rooms.
✚ F7 ✉ 65–7 Belgrave Road, SW1 ☎ 020 7834 6721, fax 020 7931 0201 🚇 Victoria

WINDERMERE HOTEL
Friendly atmosphere and elegant style.
✚ F8 ✉ 142–4 Warwick Way, SW1 ☎ 020 7834 5163, fax 020 7630 8831 🚇 Victoria

LONDON
travel facts

ARRIVING & DEPARTING

Before you go

- Check that your passport is valid for the whole length of your stay.
- Passport holders from E.U. member countries, the U.S. and some Commonwealth countries (such as Australia and Canada) do not require a visa; visitors from any other country should check.
- Write to the London Tourist Board for a free information pack ✉ 26 Grosvenor Gardens, London, SW1.

When to go

- The tourist season is year round, and almost all attractions remain open most days of the year.
- Peak season is June–September: arrive with a hotel reservation and pre-booked theater seats.
- Quietest months are January and February. Theater tickets are easier to find Monday–Thursday throughout the year.

Climate

- Officially, London is warmish in summer and coldish in winter, without extremes.
- Officially, London's rainfall is even throughout the year, rising in September and November.
- Unofficially, London's weather is unpredictable. It may be unusually mild in winter or cold in summer, and it can rain at any time. Dress in layers, and bring a raincoat.

Arriving by air

- London has five airports:

Gatwick

- Gatwick ☎ 01293 535353 is 30 miles south of Hyde Park Corner.
- Two terminals, North and South, each with information desks.
- Trains leave from South Terminal:

Gatwick Express to Victoria station (30 minutes); Thameslink trains via London Bridge, Blackfriars, and City Thameslink to King's Cross station.

- Bus services include Flightline 777, from each terminal to Victoria Coach station (at least an hour).

Heathrow

- Heathrow is 15 miles west of Hyde Park Corner, ☎ 020 8759 4321 for all airport information.
- Terminal 1 handles mostly British and continental flights; Terminal 2, continental; Terminal 3—mostly intercontinental, and Terminal 4 mostly British Airways (BA), intercontinental, Concorde, and BA's Paris and Amsterdam flights.
- All four terminals have information desks; London Tourist Board's desk is at Terminals 1, 2, and 3 underground station.
- Quickest way to London is by Heathrow Express to Paddington station, a 15 minute ride departing every 15 minutes, or the underground: two stations, one for Terminals 1, 2, and 3; one for Terminal 4 on the Piccadilly line, which goes direct to central London (South Kensington 40 minutes, King's Cross 50 minutes).
- Bus services include the two Airbus routes, A1 and A2, from all terminals to several London areas.
- A taxi from the official taxi rank will cost at least £30 to central London, even outside rush hours.

London City Airport

- ☎ 020 7646 0088 Located beside the City, so use a taxi or the two Airbus shuttles—to Canary Wharf (for Docklands Light Railway, which connects to the Underground at Bank station) or to Liverpool Street station (which also connects to the underground).

- For the business traveler; check-in time is 15 minutes before the flight.

London Luton

- ☎ 01582 405100 Located 33 miles north of central London.
- Mainly U.K. and continental flights.
- Luton Railway station is on the Thameslink to King's Cross; buses go to Victoria Coach station.

Stansted

- ☎ 01279 680500 Located 30 miles northeast of central London.
- Mostly European flights; also transatlantic flights in summer.
- Stansted Express trains run to Liverpool Street station (40 minutes).

Arriving by sea and train

- The quickest way to London from any port is usually by train, and the least expensive is often by bus.

Arriving via the Channel Tunnel

- Eurostar trains ☎ 0990 186186 are for foot passengers only. Best to book. Trains run between Waterloo International and Paris, including Disneyland Paris (3 hours), Brussels (3 hours 15 minutes), and Lille (2 hours).
- Eurotunnel ☎ 0990 353535 is for vehicles only. No reservations necessary, but fares often cheaper for advance reservations. Three times an hour between Calais and Folkestone (join the M20 to London at junction 11a), 24 hours.

Arriving by car

- London driving is slow, parking is expensive, and fines are high. Use public transportation.
- Check with your hotel about off-street parking.

Arriving by bus

- Victoria Coach station ✉ Buckingham Palace Road, SW1 ☎ 020 7730 3466/0990 808080 for information. MasterCard and Visa bookings ☎ 020 7730 3499.

Customs regulations

- No limit to goods for personal use brought by visitors from E.U. member countries.
- Limits apply for other visitors; if in doubt use the red customs channel.

Departure/airport tax

- Departure tax is currently £10, often included in the ticket price. In addition, each airport levies a service charge.

ESSENTIAL FACTS

Tourist information centers

- London Tourist Board (website: www.londontown.com) centers:
- ✉ Victoria Forecourt, SW1 🕐 Daily 8–7 (Nov–Easter: Mon–Sat 8–6; Sun 8:30–4) The largest center, with comprehensive London information and hotel booking service. Free maps for roads, buses, and Underground, plus events sheets.
- ✉ Heathrow Terminals 1, 2 and 3 underground station, Heathrow Airport 🕐 Daily 8–6
- ✉ Heathrow Termianl 3 arrivals concourse 🕐 Daily 6AM–11PM
- ✉ Liverpool Street underground station, EC2 🕐 Mon–Fri 8–8; Sat, Sun 8:45–5:30
- ✉ Waterloo International Terminus, SE1 🕐 Daily 8:30AM–10:30PM.

Local centers

- For detailed information on the City of London: City of London Information Centre ✉ St. Paul's Churchyard, EC4 ☎ 020 7332 1456 🕐 Apr–Sep: daily 9:30–5. Oct–Mar: Mon–Fri 9:30–5; Sat 9:30–12:30
- Greenwich Tourist Information Centre ✉ 46 Greenwich Church Street, Greenwich, SE10 ☎ 020 8858 6376

⊕ Daily, usually 10:15–4:45
- Discover Islington Centre ✉ 44 Duncan Street, N1 ☎ 020 7278 8787 ⊕ Apr–Oct: Mon 2–5 Tue–Sat 10–1:30, 2:30–5
- Richmond Tourist Information Centre ✉ Old Town Hall, Whittaker Avenue, Richmond, Surrey ☎ 020 8940 9125 ⊕ Mon–Fri 10–6, Sat 10–5 (May–Oct: also Sun 10:15–4:15)
- Southwark Tourist Information Centre ✉ 6 Tooley Street, SE1 ☎ 020 7403 8299 ⊕ Apr–Oct: Mon–Sat 10–6; Sun 10:30–5:30. Nov–Mar: Mon–Sat 10–4; Sun 10:30–4
- Twickenham Tourist Information Centre ✉ The Atrium, Civic Centre, York Street, Twickenham, Middlesex ☎ 020 8891 7272 ⊕ Mon–Fri 9–5.

Visitorcall
- 24-hour recorded telephone guide ☎ 0839 123456 covering over 30 subjects. Premium rates are charged. To access specific lines directly, dial 0839 123 plus 400 (what's on this week), 401 (seasonal events), 403 (exhibitions), 407 (Sundays in London), 411 (Changing the Guard), 416 (popular West End shows), 424 (where to take children), 428 (street markets), 429 (museums), 430 (traveling in London).

Hotel reservations
- The London Tourist Board ☎ 020 7604 2890 publishes an annual hotel guide, *Where to Stay in London*, and runs a hotel booking service; credit card payment only. £5 fee.
- The Automobile Association (AA) publishes an annual hotel guide (available from bookshops), *The Hotel Guide*, covering the whole of Britain with a section on London. Their hotel booking service ☎ 0870 5050505 is free for its members but a database of all AA inspected hotels can be found on their

website. To find out more about the AA, visit them on: www.theaa.co.uk.

Britain information
- Britain Visitor Centre ✉ 1 Regent Street, Piccadilly Circus, SW1 (no ☎) ⊕ Mon–Fri 9–6:30; Sat–Sun 10–4 (May–Sep: Sat 9–5)
- British Tourist Authority information service ☎ 020 8846 9000.

Opening hours
- Major attractions: seven days a week; some open late on Sun.
- Stores: six days a week; some open on Sun. For late-night shopping (► 70).
- Banks: Mon–Fri 9:30–5; a few remain open later or open on Sat mornings. Bureaux de change have longer opening hours (including weekends).
- Post offices: usually Mon–Fri 9–5:30; Sat 9–12:30.

Public holidays
- Jan 1; Good Friday; Easter Mon; May Day (first Mon in May); last Mon in May; last Mon in Aug; Dec 25; Dec 26.
- Almost all attractions and stores close Christmas Day; many close Dec 24, Jan 1, and Good Fri as well. Stores, restaurants, and attractions remain open on other holidays but it is advisable to check in advance.

Money
- 100 pence to £1. Coins: 1p, 2p, 5p, 10p, 20p, 50p £1, and £2; bills: £5, £10, £20, and £50. Collectors' £2 coins can be bought at banks.
- Bureaux de change offer the best exchange rate. Check rates, commission, and other charges.
- The euro currency was adopted by most E.U. countries in 1999; Britain remains an exception.

Tipping

- 10 percent for restaurants, taxis, hairdressers, and other services. Look over restaurants checks to see if service charge has already been added or is included.
- No tipping in theaters, cinemas, concert halls or in pubs and bars (unless there is waitress service).

Places of worship

- Almost every denomination is represented. Refer to the Yellow Pages telephone directory.

Time

- G.M.T. (Greenwich Mean Time) is standard time; B.S.T. (British Summer Time: late March to late October) is one hour ahead.

Electricity

- Standard supply is 240V.
- Motor-driven equipment needs a specific frequency; in the U.K. it is 50 cycles per second (kHz).

PUBLIC TRANSPORTATION

London Transport travel information centers

- Centers sell travel passes and provide underground and train maps, bus route maps, and information on cheap tickets.
- 🕐 Daily at each terminal at Heathrow Airport and at the following stations:
  🚇 Hammersmith, Oxford Circus (except Sun) Piccadilly Circus, St. James's Park (except Sun), and Heathrow Terminals 1, 2 and 3
  🚆 Victoria, Euston, King's Cross, Paddington
- London Transport inquiries telephone service ☎ 020 7222 1234 (🕐 24 hours); 020 7222 1200.

Travel passes

- Priced according to length of validity and how many of the six London zones it covers, a pass usually pays for itself within two or three journeys. There are three main types.
- Travelcards: valid after 9:30AM for unlimited travel by underground, British Rail, Docklands Light Railway, and most buses; sold at travel information centers, British Rail stations, all underground stations, and some stores (such as newspaper shops); cover travel for one day, a week, a weekend, a month or a year. Adults need a photocard (except for a one-day travelcard), sold at travel information centers; children aged 5–15 pay child fares but need a child-rate photocard; children under five travel free.
- Bus passes: bus-only passes are on sale at travel information centers, underground stations, and some newspaper shops.
- Visitor travelcards: similar to travelcards but no need for a photo; valid for one, three, four, or seven days. Must be bought before arrival in London.

The underground (the tube)

- Eleven color-coded lines link almost 300 stations. Use a travel pass or buy a ticket from a machine (some give change) or ticket booth; keep the ticket until the end of the journey. The system includes the Docklands Light Railway (DLR; between Tower Gateway station and Lewisham, via Greenwich). The Jubilee line extension reaches Greenwich Peninsula.

Buses

- Plan your journey using the latest copy of the *All London Bus Guide*, available at tourist offices (► 89–90).
- A bus stop is indicated by a red sign on a metal pole.

- On a two-man bus, the conductor comes to inspect the travel pass or sell a ticket; on a one-man bus, the driver inspects passes or sells tickets as passengers board—try to have the exact change.

Taxis

- Drivers of official (mostly black) cabs know the city well. They are obliged to follow the shortest route unless an alternative is agreed. A taxi is licensed for up to four passengers.
- Hail only taxis with the yellow "For Hire" light on; tell the driver the destination before getting in.
- Meter charges increase in the evenings and on weekends.
- Avoid minicabs; they may have no meter and inadequate insurance.
- Black cabs can be ordered by telephone: Computer Cab ☎ 020 7286 0286; Radio Taxis ☎ 020 7272 0272.

MEDIA & COMMUNICATIONS

Telephones

- Check the mark-up rate before making a call from a hotel.
- London numbers (now 8 digits) are prefixed with the code 020 when dialing from outside the city.
- Use coins or a British Telecom (BT) phonecard to call from BT phone booths. Phonecards are sold at post offices and news stands. Many phones take credit cards.
- Information ☎ 192
- Operator ☎ 100 to check costs, call collect, or call another person in the U.K. via the operator.
- International telephoning: ☎ 153 for directory enquiries; ☎ 155 to call collect.
- Beware of high charges on some premium rate numbers (prefixed 09) and special rate (08) numbers.

Sending a letter or a postcard

- Stamps are sold at post offices and some newsstands and stores.
- Trafalgar Square Post Office stays open till late: ✉ William IV Street, WC2 ⊙ Mon–Sat 8–8
- Mailboxes are red.

Newspapers & magazines

- Quality papers include *The Times*, the *Financial Times*, the *Daily Telegraph*, the *Independent*, the *Guardian* and, on Sundays, the *Sunday Times*, *Sunday Telegraph*, *Observer* and *Independent on Sunday*.
- London's only evening paper, the *Evening Standard* (Mon–Fri), first edition out around noon, is strong on entertainment and nightlife.
- *Time Out* (published weekly on Wednesdays) lists almost everything going.

Television

- BBC 1 (varied); BBC 2 (more cultural); ITV (commercial—varied); Channel 4 (commercial—cultural and minority interest); Channel 5 (commercial—varied); satellite and cable channels (mainly in larger hotels) include CNN, MTV, and Sky. A few provide digital T.V.

EMERGENCIES

Sensible precautions

- Do not wear valuables that can be snatched. If you must bring valuables, put them in a hotel or bank safe box.
- Make a note of all passport, ticket, and credit card numbers, and keep it in a separate place.
- Keep money, passport, and credit cards in a fully closed bag. Carry only a small amount of cash and keep it out of sight.
- Keep your bag in sight at all times—do not sling it over your

back or put it on the floor of a café, pub, or cinema. Keep an eye on your coat, hat, umbrella, and shopping bags.
- At night, try not to travel alone; if you must, either pre-book a taxi or keep to well-lit streets and use a bus or underground train where there are already other people.

Lost credit cards
- Report any loss immediately to the relevant company and to the nearest police station; also call your bank.
- To discover your credit card company's local 24-hour emergency number ☎ 192 (information).

Medical treatment
- E.U. nationals and citizens of some other countries with special arrangements (Australia and New Zealand) may receive free National Health Service (NHS) medical treatment. Others pay.
- If you need an ambulance ☎ 999 on any telephone, free of charge.
- NHS hospitals with 24-hour emergency departments include: University College Hospital ✉ Gower Street (entrance in Grafton Way), WC1 ☎ 020 7387 9300; Chelsea and Westminster Hospital ✉ 369 Fulham Road, SW10 ☎ 020 8746 8000
- Private hospitals, with no emergency unit, include the Cromwell Hospital ✉ Cromwell Road, SW5 ☎ 020 7460 2000
- Great Chapel Street Medical Centre ✉ 13 Great Chapel Street, W1 ☎ 020 7437 9360 is an NHS clinic open to all, but visitors from countries without the NHS reciprocal agreement must pay.
- Dental specialist: contact British Dental Association ☎ 020 7935 0875 ext 222 for Helpline
- Eye specialist: Moorfields Eye

Hospital ✉ City Road, EC1 ☎ 020 7253 3411; Dolland & Aitchison ✉ 229–31 Regent Street, W1 ☎ 020 7499 8777 (opticians and on-site workshop for glasses and contact lenses).
- For homeopathic pharmacies, practitioners, and advice: the British Homoeopathic Association ✉ 27a Devonshire Street, W1 ☎ 020 7935 2163.

Medicines
- Many drugs cannot be bought over the counter. For an NHS prescription, pay a modest flat rate; if a private doctor prescribes, you pay the full cost. To claim charges back on insurance, keep receipts.
- Drugstores open late include: Bliss Chemist ✉ 5 Marble Arch, W1 ☎ 020 7723 6116 🕐 Daily 9AM–midnight
- Ainsworth's Homeopathic Pharmacy ✉ 38 New Cavendish Street ☎ 020 7935 5330 🕐 Mon–Fri 9–5:30; Sat 9–4.

Emergency telephone numbers
- For police, fire, or ambulance, ☎ 999 from any telephone, free of charge. The call goes directly to the emergency services. Tell the operator which street you are on and the nearest landmark, intersection or house number; stay by the telephone until help arrives.

Embassies & missions
- Australian High Commission ✉ Australia House, Strand, WC2 ☎ 020 7379 4334
- Canadian High Commission ✉ 38 Grosvenor Street, W1 ☎ 020 7258 6600
- Irish Embassy ✉ 17 Grosvenor Place, SW1 ☎ 020 7235 2171
- New Zealand High Commission ✉ New Zealand House, 80 Haymarket, SW1 ☎ 020 7930 8422
- Embassy of the United States of America ✉ Grosvenor Square, W1 ☎ 020 7499 9000.

INDEX

Citypack
London

Important note

Time inevitably brings changes, so always confirm prices, travel facts, and other perishable information when it matters. Although Fodor's cannot accept responsibility for errors, you can use this guide in the confidence that we have taken every care to ensure its accuracy.

Published in the United States by Fodor's Travel Publications, Inc.
Published in the United Kingdom by AA Publishing

Fodor's is a registered trademark of Random House, Inc.

ISBN 0–679–00482–3
Third Edition

FODOR'S CITYPACK LONDON

AUTHOR *Louise Nicholson*
THIRD EDITION UPDATED BY *Louise Nicholson*
"WHERE TO..." SECTION UPDATED BY *Elizabeth Carter*
CARTOGRAPHY *The Automobile Association*
                       RV Reise- und Verkehrsverlag
COVER DESIGN *Tigist Getachew, Fabrizio La Rocca*
INDEXER *Marie Lorimer*

Acknowledgments

The Automobile Association would like to thank the following photographers, libraries and associations for their assistance in the preparation of this book.
© BRITISH MUSEUM 43 COURTAULD GALLERY 41 LONDON AQUARIUM 51 NATIONAL PORTRAIT GALLERY 38a, 38b REX FEATURES LTD 9 SCIENCE MUSEUM 27 SPECTRUM COLOUR LIBRARY 13b, 29, 32. All remaining pictures are held in the Association's own library (AA PHOTO LIBRARY) with contributions from: P. BAKER 7, 45b; D. FORSS 2; S. & O. MATHEWS 46b; R. MORT 13a, 18, 48b, 54, 61a; B. SMITH 24a, 24b, 30b, 35a, 40a; R. STRANGE 6, 23b, 25, 26a, 26b, 28a, 28b, 30a, 31, 44, 46a, 47, 49a, 49b, 50, 58, 60, 87b; M. TRELAWNY 16, 21, 42a, 56; R. VICTOR 23a; W. VOYSEY 1, 12, 17, 33b, 35b, 36, 40b, 48a, 57; P. WILSON 5a, 39, 53, 87a; T. WOODCOCK 33a, 34, 37b, 45a, 55.

Special sales

Fodor's Travel Publications are available at special discounts for bulk purchases (100 copies or more) for sales promotions or premiums. Special editions, including personalized covers, excerpts of existing guides, and corporate imprints, can be created in large quantities for special needs. For more information, contact your local bookseller or write to Special Markets, Fodor's Travel Publications, 201 East 50th Street, New York, NY 10022. Inquiries from Canada should be directed to your local Canadian bookseller or sent to Random House of Canada, Ltd., Marketing Department, 2775 Matheson Blvd. East, Mississauga, Ontario L4W 4P7.

Color separation by Daylight Colour Art Pte Ltd, Singapore
Manufactured by Dai Nippon Printing Co. (Hong Kong) Ltd
10 9 8 7 6 5 4 3 2 1

Titles in the Citypack series

- Amsterdam ● Atlanta ● Beijing ● Berlin ● Boston ● Chicago ● Dublin ●
- Florence ● Hong Kong ● London ● Los Angeles ● Miami ● Montreal ●
- New York ● Paris ● Prague ● Rome ● San Francisco ● Seattle ● Shanghai ●
- Sydney ● Tokyo ● Toronto ● Venice ● Washington, D.C. ●